YES
YOU
Freakin'
CAN

YES
YOU

CAN

BE BETTER THAN YOU
THOUGHT POSSIBLE

Trevor Lynch

ISBN PAPERBACK# – 978-2-9580613-0-2
ISBN ELECTRONIC# – 978-2-9580613-2-6

Printed in the United States of America.

Trefle Rebels

www.trevorlynch.net

For Alexia and Malorie.

I love you more than you'll ever know.

CONTENTS

PART 3:
SO WHAT NEXT?

YES
YOU
Freakin'
CAN

INTRODUCTION

We sat at our bedroom window in the Bellagio Hotel on the Las Vegas strip, mesmerized by the breathtaking view of the water fountains dancing to the rhythm of the music and light show outside. The mockup of the Eiffel tower across the street looked life size. It was a hot evening in early July, and still the strip was full of tourists like us, trying to soak up the ambience and all the other crazy stuff this city had to offer.

This was possibly the last vacation I would have with my two beautiful daughters, Alexia and Malorie. They were both grown at this point, aged 18 and 20, and I wanted it to be special and memorable. In addition to seeing Vegas, we stayed with one of my childhood friends and his lovely family in LA, rented an American SUV, cycled the Manhattan Beach boardwalk, strolled around Beverly Hills, took in the craziness of Venice Beach, and hiked up to the Hollywood Sign.

On the surface, things couldn't have been better. Under the surface, it was a completely different story.

Sitting at that window, thoughts crept in about the virtual interview I had lined up for the following morning, for a team coaching role based in Switzerland. It sounded really exciting, and it was something I was looking forward to.

If only the timing could have been different. I was feeling torn up inside and lost as to what the future would be like. My girlfriend of two years had just left me, and my manager had just recently informed me that my job would be disappearing at the end of the year, being moved to a lower-cost location. On top of that, around the time I was informed about my job loss, I had just signed the papers to sell my house to a neighboring restaurant owner, so I wouldn't have a place of my own in a couple of months. Without a job, I wouldn't be eligible for a house loan, and I'd have to go back to renting again, something I promised myself I would no longer do. My self-confidence was low, and I felt empty inside. Each of these events was challenging by itself, but all three combined had my head spinning and unfocused. I love my daughters dearly, and I wanted to be close to them, so I didn't want to be forced to move far away for another job.

Sitting in silence, I asked myself: *How can I get focused on tomorrow morning's interview, which could open up exciting new possibilities in my career? How can I get into the best possible mindset for this great opportunity, which will also allow me to stay close to them?*

Have you ever wished there was a magic formula for overcoming the stress or pressure that arises when you need to perform at your best? Have you ever struggled to overcome internal doubts that cause your mind to focus on everything that could go wrong? It could be right before a big presentation, a job interview, asking someone special out on a date, or just before the start of a sporting event. Your brain unexpectedly makes you more aware of your flaws, you doubt your abilities, and your confidence plummets. As a result, you leave the event feeling like you could have done better. If only you could have been your best self, that more confident and radiant you who would have smashed this.

What would it mean for your self-esteem, career, relationships, and future if you could always show up exactly as you wanted or needed to, in order to maximize your chances of getting your desired outcome? Imagine the impact if you could, like a light switch, turn on your best version of you, almost at will, with only a few minutes of preparation. Think about it for a few seconds.

Part 1 of this book will show you how to set specific intentions for how you want to show up and get your subconscious to work with you, rather than against you, to make it happen. When done correctly, the techniques will not only get you to your best, but can also help you exceed what you believe you are capable of.

What about when you are going through a rough patch or when life knocks you down and you need to get back to a positive energy place quickly?

Life has a habit of throwing challenges our way that test our level of resilience, our ability to bounce back strong after being knocked down. **Part 2** of the book will focus on how to best prepare for this, as well as how to not only get back on your feet but become a better version of yourself as a result of the experience.

Following the exercises contained in each chapter will help you get through some of life's most difficult moments and bounce back stronger.

Part 3 of the book focuses on what to do after getting yourself to a better, stronger you in Parts 1 and 2. It includes taking a strategic look at all areas of your life, realizing where you are now on the journey, and deciding what you will focus on next to have more balance and fulfilment. The beauty in your life will be more visible, and you will be more focused on creating more memorable moments for yourself and those you care about.

I'm confident that this stuff works! I've tried every technique in this book, both on myself and with others. I've taught and coached people from all walks of life, who used these strategies to achieve their goals, outperform their expectations, and strengthen their self-belief and resilience.

Some used them to give incredible presentations despite having a debilitating fear of public speaking due to a past experience, while others used them to score from a very unlikely position in a match, speak up at important meetings, be confident and composed in job interviews, succeed during an exam, have more confident first dates, perform better in the bedroom, and stand strong and keep advancing in the face of life's challenges.

The techniques are so simple and so effective—yet most of us are unaware of them because we were never taught them in school and may not have encountered them in our professional lives.

I became aware of these techniques several years ago, when I was looking for something to help me become a better version of myself, after life threw several difficult challenges my way. I researched all I could find from authors, coaches, and life strategists on how to do this, and I designed what worked best for me and the people I've coached and taught. I've tested, experimented with, and refined these techniques for easy and effective application in this how-to guide.

It is my honor to have the opportunity to assist you in taking your belief in what you're capable of, your self-esteem, and life quality to the next level. My promise to you is that if you practice the exercises that work best for you, from those I have included in the following chapters, you will move the needle on what is possible for you in life.

It was the morning of the interview. I sat on my bed in the Vegas hotel room, wondering what I could do. My daughters, asleep in their beds, were oblivious to my dilemma. They didn't need to know about it. It was my stuff to deal with, and up to me to find a solution. I was looking inside of myself for inspiration. Again, I wondered: *How can I get my mind in the right place to have a great interview?* Finally, it came to me. The answer lay in what I often do to get myself in the zone for an important event. How could I not have thought of that? The stress related to those challenging events caused me to lose focus and not think of it until now, the 11th hour.

In the silence of the early morning, I got to it and ran through a couple of targeted visualizations and affirmations to mentally prepare for the interview. After all, worked for me in the past in almost all challenging situations where I knew the outcome I wanted in advance.

This got me completely in the zone, just when I needed it. The interview went precisely as I had imagined it would go. Or, rather, I behaved exactly as I had visualized in my mind's eye.

I was composed, focused, and strategic in my communication. "So did you get the job?" I hear you ask. I didn't, and it was OK. I interviewed really well, and there was someone else who had more relevant experience for that role, someone I know, in fact, and I was really happy for her.

Initially, I did feel a level of disappointment that I wasn't selected and went through a period where I was somewhat concerned about what I would do next. However, my positive interview gave me the self-confidence I needed, as did reframing the situation. My self-talk went from: "How many more positions will I be turned down for?" to "I know that role wasn't for me. There is something better out there—more suited to what I do best and what I want to do more of."

I have since been proposed a role in the same organization, and I'm happily continuing to work in the field of people development.

A few weeks after returning from Vegas, the buyer pulled out at the very last minute. I didn't have to move. Concerning my ex-girlfriend, I adopted a mindset of gratitude. I realized that we spent valuable time together but there was someone else out there for me who would be a better match. I just needed to continue my path until I found her.

What worked best for me through this challenging period are some of what we'll cover in the chapters ahead, including Targeted Visualization, focusing on my Wow List, gratitude practice, creating my Victory List, using strong affirmations, reframing, and bouncing forward.

Okay, are you ready to do some of this in your own life and expand what's possible for you?

PART 1

YOUR BEST SELF
FOR ANY CHALLENGE
OR GOAL

CHAPTER 1

———

Where Are You at Right Now?

*"It's not because things are difficult that we do not dare,
it's because we do not dare that things are difficult."*
— Seneca

Vincent, a very competent and well-travelled marketing professional, in his mid-forties, was passionate about tennis. He had been playing for a few years and was winning friendly tennis matches in his club on a regular basis but couldn't win a single match in any open competition. He was becoming obsessed with finding out how he could turn it around. His tennis coach and fellow club members told him to persist, and that the more tournaments he entered, the more used to playing in competition he would be, and the wins would come. It sounded like great advice, but nope, that didn't do it for him. He then changed his racket for a heavier one, on advice from more seasoned players, but to no avail. Next, again, on good advice, he had a warm-up game just prior to commencing the upcoming tournament match, and still the same result. He lost one more time to a player whom he believed he was capable of beating. He considered the possibility that the other players who had beaten him were just better than him, but he was certain that wasn't the case. He became very frustrated with his situation and was convinced that his problem was psychological.

He was right. It all came down to his mindset. He desperately wanted to win his next match in order to boost his confidence, self-esteem, and the respect of his teammates. Finally, Vincent won, not just his next tennis match, but the entire tournament, and he's still doing it today. All down to a few simple and effective techniques that flipped his mindset and had him show up and perform at his best.

What's challenging for you?

Vincent almost stopped competing in his favorite sport, believing that he wasn't made for it. How about you? What is it that's challenging for you? For Vincent, who is successful at most other things in his life, it happened to be tennis.

Consider what it would mean for you, your self-esteem, and certain areas of your life if you could raise the bar on how you show up and perform, by 10, 20, or 50 percent with some simple and effective techniques. Before we look at how you can accomplish this, first select a tangible challenge for you to apply this to. Where in your life do you want to put your best foot forward, or go above and beyond what you currently believe you're capable of?

What stressful challenge or goal do you have in your personal life or career right now, or that's coming up soon? The stress related to your challenge may be due to a past bad experience in a similar situation, or the fact that it's something new for you, or that the stakes are high, or because this type of event or challenge feels outside your comfort zone at the moment. Typical challenges I've seen include…

☐ Making an important presentation or speech
☐ Going on a first date

- ☐ A job interview for a long-awaited career move
- ☐ A sports competition
- ☐ Speaking up in a meeting with senior managers / stakeholders / customers
- ☐ Spending that first romantic night with a new partner
- ☐ Starting a new job
- ☐ Looking to make a great first impression
- ☐ Taking an exam for a professional qualification
- ☐ Being confident in certain settings or with certain people

If you don't have a challenge in mind right now, ask yourself what you've always wanted to try but keep putting off, because you're telling yourself all the reasons why you can't do it or be it. Then, consider making that your exciting personal challenge.

Once you've selected your personal challenge, choose a phrase from the list below that best represents how you feel about it.

- ☐ I'd do anything I can to avoid it
- ☐ I get butterflies when I think of it
- ☐ I'm really not looking forward to it
- ☐ I'm feeling a little uncomfortable about it
- ☐ It doesn't really bother me
- ☐ I have all the confidence I need

Before we proceed and discuss how to show up and be at your best, or to exceed what you believe to be your best, let's first assess your level of motivation to improve. This is crucial in determining whether you will use the techniques in this part of the book or if you will simply read on. This, in turn, will influence how you'll feel about yourself in the future and if, when, or to what level you will succeed in this area.

Where would you say your level of motivation is, right now, to perform at your best for the situation or challenge you've chosen?

1. Pretty low. I'll just do what I always do and get the same old results.

2. Average. I'm interested in knowing how to be more confident in the situation.
3. High. I'd like to change my approach in order to achieve a better result.
4. Extremely high. I really want to be better than I have been previously or than I believe I'm capable of and am eager to learn how and apply it.

If you're at level 1 and your typical results are at the level you set for yourself, that's fantastic. I congratulate you and propose you to pick another challenge that will push you out of your comfort zone. Basically, if you're not rating your motivation as a 3 or a 4, then I urge you to consider an alternative challenge, one where your level of motivation to show up as your best you is higher.

Remember that confidence in our abilities is often situational, so choose a situation in which you are less confident and could use a boost.

OK, cool! You've identified your personal challenge, are aware of your feelings about it, and are motivated to "knock it out of the park."

Your Personal Assistant

You may not be aware of it, but you have a personal assistant to help you succeed with your personal challenge. His name is RAS, and he's always with you. RAS has a permanent residence in a part of your brain, and his full name is Reticular Activating System. His function is to highlight, or make your conscious brain aware of, anything related to whatever is important to you, or that is part of your world. You'll want to engage him as you read this book so he will highlight to you whatever stories, techniques, and tips you should pay special attention to in order to succeed. For that to happen, you must clearly define your personal challenge so RAS is aware of it. To ensure it's clear for RAS, capture it in writing in the space below.

My personal challenge / goal is...

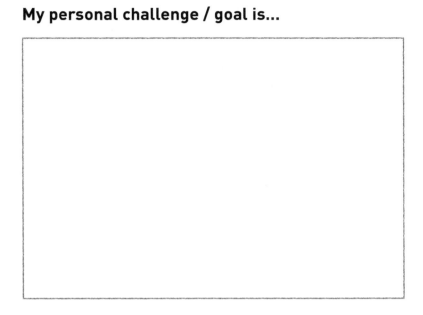

Now that RAS is aware of your personal challenge, he's on it. Let me demonstrate how he operates with a couple of examples.

For those of you who have recently purchased a new car, did you start seeing that particular model car everywhere after you bought or decided on it? I mean a lot more than you used to. I bet that yes, you did. Were there really more than there had been before? In most cases, no. So their number didn't change much around the time you first drove yours or you decided on that model.

The thing is, your eyes saw them all the time, but your brain did not. When RAS realized that this particular car became important for you, or became part of your world, he brought your attention to whatever was related to it. Hence you see more of them on the road. He previously filtered them out, as there was no obvious reason for you to pay attention to them.

Those of you who have children most likely experienced a similar phenomenon. When you or your partner became pregnant or decided to become pregnant, I'm sure you started seeing babies, toddlers, strollers, and baby-related advertisements everywhere. That

13

was RAS at work. Babies had not been a part of your life up until that point. As a result, even though your eyes saw them, your brain did not. Up to that point, babies were not part of your world and not something you had decided on having yet, so RAS didn't bring your attention to baby-related stuff.

For those of you who don't have cars or children, it could be a specific pair of sneakers or a dress. You started seeing a lot more of those around once that particular dress or those exact sneakers became a part of your world.

Like most great assistants, RAS doesn't want to needlessly have you focusing on something that's not important to you. He will only make you aware of those things that he knows are relevant to what's important to you.

RAS is incredible and never has an off day. He is always at work, ensuring that not every piece of information you see or hear will get through. As well as him wanting to optimize your time and energy, he knows you'd go crazy if you had to process every single piece of information that your senses detect. Take a look around you right now and consider all of the details that your brain would have to take in on a continuous basis if it didn't have RAS being an incredible filter.

Here's some of what my senses are picking up right now...

I'm seeing bamboo plants that look like they have an evening thirst, rooted in large earth-colored pottery pots, a Bordeaux-leafed Japanese maple growing in the front corner of my house, the soil around it gently covered in white pebbles to protect it from drying when the temperature goes above 85 degrees, the uneven cobble-stones of various shades that make up my terrace, a few pine trees planted around the neighboring hotel, the wooden fence that delimits the open terrace of the nearby restaurant, the sky-blue leather-covered notebook poised for use next to my laptop, which is sitting on a black-sprayed wrought-iron table...and the list goes on.

And that is only the visual list! In the air is the scent of freshly cooked French Muenster cheese, hot pizza straight from a neighbor's oven, humidity from a recent downpour of rain...and I'm hearing a mix of conversations in several languages, at varying volumes and intensities, all audible despite the soothing sound of Melodia Africana playing through my iPhone earpiece, which is my attempt to drown out the distracting nearby buzz and advance this book for you.

Take a look around you. What are all the details you're seeing now that your brain normally just scans over? What sounds are you hearing? What perfumes or odors are floating around in the air?

RAS's purpose is to screen what's not relevant and highlight what is important for you to notice. Now that he knows your personal challenge, as you read through these chapters, you will start to notice examples, exercises, or stories that you may otherwise skip over. They will be most useful for you and relevant to your goal. Thank you, RAS!

Time is your challenge?

As well as getting RAS on the case, the key to getting maximum benefit from the chapters ahead for your challenge is doing the activities, developing new skills, and putting them into practice.

My goal is for you to be, or to show up as, the best version of you when you most need to. Reading alone won't change your outcomes. Just knowing what to do is so simple in today's digital age. Google or YouTube will describe what you can do for most challenges in a matter of minutes. Taking action and actually using what you learn is what will lead to more of what you desire.

Allow me to ask you a direct question. Have you ever read a book about how to improve something in your life, found it interesting and, dare I say, even practical, but never put any of the super effective ideas and techniques into action? It could have been a book on losing weight, getting in shape, improving your memory, strengthening your communication skills, or working on your relationship. I know I'm guilty of it. How about you?

Or you went to a class for a day or two, and when you returned to work, you filed away the class notes, you told your coworkers how interesting it was, how delicious the lunch food was, the discussions you had with interesting people, and never followed through on the actions proposed in class?

Whenever I've asked this question to a class of adults, even those most well-educated, the majority of them have raised their hands, admitting to being guilty of the same. Why is that?

According to what I've heard from others, and my own experience, we resort to excuses like the age-old "I don't have time." Hmmm, that's interesting.

If that's the case for you, imagine the following... You have the same hectic schedule as you do now, with little time for anything else, and you've just won a new high-end sports car worth up to $200,000.

The problem is that you only have one week to test drive each car, choose the model you prefer, and drive away in your new sports car with a gleaming smile on your face. Remember that you have the same hectic schedule as you do now!

Will you be able to make the time? That's a tough one, isn't it? :-)

Surely, you'll find a way to make it happen. You'll rearrange your schedule or decline a few meeting invitations, let go of less important or less urgent matters, and eagerly go test drive these beauties.

So, what's the difference?

You say, "Well, the difference is that I get the car of a lifetime."

Yes, I agree with you.

And what does that represent? "My image, my trips to the coast, what I'll do on weekends, how I'll feel, and a bunch of other exciting aspects of my life!" you exclaim.

So, how the new car makes feel provides you with the energy, motivation, and creativity to now find the time. To put it succinctly: It's more important to choose and drive away in a free brand-new sports car than to follow the advice in that book you read or the class you took? That's why you'll be able to find the time.

In other words, obtaining that free high-end sports car became such a high priority that you felt compelled to devote sufficient time to it. Now we're getting somewhere.

The main reason I bet you didn't take a recommended action to improve whatever it was in your life that you wanted to improve, or at least wish would be better, is that you didn't have a compelling enough reason why. Not that you didn't have time, though that's a great classic response that we all hide behind at times in the comfort of believing that one day, when we have all this time available, we might get back to this. That is, of course, if nothing else is more important at that time in the future.

This is perfectly normal.

Try something new this time!

Let's begin by understanding why it's a priority for you to show up at your best for your personal challenge. While it may not appear as cool as a new sports car initially, it will make you feel incredible about yourself and what you're capable of, boost your confidence in your abilities, and expand your beliefs about what you are capable of achieving. Once actualized, this can be considerably more valuable than a sports car! In the space below, or in your journal, write down what you will gain if this event or challenge goes extremely well and how you will feel about yourself as a result.

My challenge / goal

What I will gain

How I'll feel about myself and what I'm capable of once I tackle this challenge successfully

CHAPTER 2

If You Believed You Could ...

*"If you want something new, you have
to stop doing something old."*
— Peter F. Drucker

The decisions that you've made, or didn't make, up to this point in your life have shaped it into what it is now. Some of them were great decisions based on empowering beliefs about yourself, your potential, and your self worth. Others were poor choices that may have stemmed from beliefs that were holding you back.

I remember leaving secondary school, which is Irish lingo for high school, trying to decide what to go on to study. I was 17 years old and had a real interest in fitness and nutrition. Back then, studying nutrition meant traveling to Scotland or another part of the UK, as there was nothing closer to home. I had never traveled much and was apprehensive about living "so far away." As these words appear on my screen, I cringe because they seem ridiculous now. It was just a short flight away.

I grew up in a working-class family with no role models to help me understand the possibilities; no well-educated or successful people around me to help a young person gain confidence or be resourceful and find solutions.

What sound like excuses now were, in fact, my past beliefs. I imagined that being separated from my family and friends would make me feel lonely and sad. I used to believe that only rich people could travel to go away to college (this was before traveling by plane became accessible cost-wise to the masses in Ireland). I reasoned that it would be better for me to stay in my hometown and pursue another path. I basically believed, rightly or wrongly, that I wouldn't be able to survive on my own in a foreign country with limited resources. So, what did I decide to do?

In a nutshell, I ended up studying engineering because that was "where the jobs were." It was a time of economic hardship, and ensuring that I qualified for a job became the ultimate factor in my decision. This was during a time when even finding a temporary job in a bar or restaurant was near impossible.

My studies lasted five years, and I despised every minute. I wasn't technically oriented, and my friends would laugh at the mention of me studying in this field. "Engineering? Really?!" I'm so grateful that today I'm in a completely different field. I'm oriented toward people and enabling them to advance to the next level or unleash potential they didn't know they had.

I chose a route less suited to my passions at the time, all because my beliefs, not facts, guided my decision-making process.

Do I regret my choice? Yes and no. My journey helped me break into the professional world, provided me with opportunities to travel, and was one of the steps that led me to where I am now. At the same time, my career would have been more interesting and fulfilling if I had believed enough in myself to go with what I was passionate about.

How have your beliefs shaped your life?

Let's focus on your journey. Where are you at in your life right now?

It's valuable to consider the decisions you've made in your life and boost your awareness about your associated beliefs. They could be related to who you had or have as a partner, how long you've been with them, where you are in your career, where you live, how you choose to present yourself, how you feel about your physical health, how alluring your goals are, the size of your previous goals, and so on.

In the table below, or in your journal, capture the main decisions you've made in your life. These are the decisions and beliefs that have shaped your life up to this point, that brought you to where you are now. Some of them were great decisions based on empowering beliefs about yourself, your potential, and your value or your worth. Others may have been poor choices that stemmed from beliefs that were holding you back.

What was the belief behind each decision that you did or didn't make?

Life Area	Decision	Empowering Beliefs Behind the Decision	Disempowering Beliefs Behind the Decision
Career	Make a move to the area of people development	It's where I excel, it gives me energy, and it feels right.	
Relationship	To stay (too long) with someone who was not a good fit for me		I couldn't find someone better

Over to you...

By this point, you can see that your life up until this moment has been largely determined by your decisions, which, in turn, have been largely determined by your beliefs about the world and, in particular, your beliefs about yourself. These beliefs include what you are, what you are not, what you can and cannot do, how you think others perceive you, how intelligent or talented you are, what will happen if you "attempt" something new, and all the other things you believe you are or are not capable of.

So, if your life to this point has been largely the result of your past beliefs, then guess what? The beliefs you hold today will have a significant impact on the next chapters of your life.

What is a belief?

A belief is something you feel certain about, whether or not it's actually true. Beliefs may change over time with new experiences, or they may remain stable. In a conversation or a coaching session, I frequently ask people, "Is that a story or a fact?" One way a belief shows up is through a story, and based on what I've observed, we tell ourselves a lot of stories about ourselves and what we say we'll never be able to accomplish.

Our conscious beliefs, or those over which we have conscious control, are frequently empowering beliefs. Those beliefs are the ones which we attempt to have or choose to have. One example is, "I believe I can be a successful online entrepreneur and live where I wish."

There are also beliefs that we hold on a subconscious level, and when there is a conflict between these subconscious beliefs and the conscious ones, the subconscious beliefs often take precedence. If your subconscious belief is, in this example, that you could never work without the security of a company structure around you, this may prevent you from ever starting your own business, online or other. This can seriously derail your plans without you even being aware of the reason why.

I believed, for example, that because I wasn't 25 anymore, and my body shape was not something I could change, due to the aging process, how I looked was just how I was. As I glanced in the mirror and saw myself getting a little flabby around the chest and belly, my subconscious belief was that it was normal.

Wondering what I could do about it, I looked for proof of the contrary. I asked myself, "What proof do I have that even at 50, I can really influence my body shape?" I sat down and wrote everything out. With self-reflection and research, I came up with the following:

□ Actor Daniel Craig, who is possibly the best James Bond yet, is one year older than me and he's in freakin' incredible shape.

□ I learned from health experts that how we eat and drink determines our body fat more so than other factors. I admit I've been eating and drinking more for pleasure than health, hence the recent chest and belly flab.

□ My father is in great shape in his seventies, so it must not be a genetic thing.

□ Before and after photos and stories of men and women, of all ages, who were way more overweight than me, showed how they transformed their bodies and health by making lifestyle changes.

As a result, I no longer believe my current body shape is primarily determined by age or genetics, but rather by my lifestyle. I now believe that as I change my lifestyle—how I eat, drink, and move my body—I take back control of my body shape. It's now back in the realm of the possible for me, whereas with my initial limiting belief, I didn't feel like going for the body shape I desired because I believed it was out of my control. Because I didn't believe it was possible, I didn't try.

Our beliefs are powerful. "How powerful?" you might ask. Two words can demonstrate this. Placebo Effect. This is basically the mind's ability to heal the body or, to put it another way, it's what the mind believes that heals the body. It's so powerful that any new drug undergoing efficacy testing must outperform the placebo by a certain margin. The drug must be able to outperform the level of healing that occurs solely as a result of our beliefs.

If our beliefs can heal the body of disease or ailments, imagine what else they can do.

Activity: **Flip Your Limiting Beliefs**

1. In the space below, or in your journal, write out the main belief you have about yourself that is holding you back from succeeding your personal challenge.

2. Note the impact it's had on your life or career. What impact is it having on you now, and if you don't change it, what will be the impact going forward if you continue to hold this belief?

3. Flip your belief to one that will empower you, and write it out in a strong positive sentence. My new empowering belief is...

4. Reflect on and write all you can think of that disproves your limiting belief and demonstrates your new empowering belief. Do this from a strong posture, possibly while nodding your head in agreement with each point.

Disproves Limiting Belief	Demonstrates New Belief

5. Read what you have in the following order. "I used to believe X, now I believe Y, and my proof is XYZ...." Find a place where you can say it aloud to yourself.

6. Sit in a strong and comfortable position and close your eyes. Relax and focus on the flow of your breath for a minute or two while allowing your eyelids to feel light. See yourself living your new belief and step into the main proof points, seeing each of them adding power to this new belief. In your mind, see them big, bold, and in color. Feel this new belief inside of you and nod your head as you do.

7. As things crop up that continue to disprove your limiting belief and demonstrate your new empowering belief, add them to your list and keep repeating steps 5 and 6.

The three-letter word that changes everything

I'm referring to that short, powerful "Y" word that can make all the difference in our beliefs and stories. It's the word "yet." Let me demonstrate what I mean.

Instead of saying "I can't dance salsa..."

Let's make a slight though powerful modification.

Try this instead… "I can't dance salsa yet."

It's a completely different perspective that gives a very different energy inside.

Instead of "I can't go on vacation on my own," try "I am not ready to go on vacation on my own yet."

The "yet" word is one of the most powerful but underutilized words concerning our beliefs about ourselves. Yes, that's also a belief. Try it now with one of your limiting beliefs about your personal challenge, or something you would like to be able to do or become. Add the word "yet" to your limiting belief. What is it you haven't been able to do up to this point in your life?

Now, read your initial limiting belief aloud. Then read the same belief with "yet" added in.

Feel how that feels inside. Can you feel the difference when you add this to a limiting belief that you have?

For me, I describe it as opening a door I previously thought was closed for me. If not fully, then at least enough to put my foot in there. I feel the possibility building up inside of me as I see it with that slight difference. Can you feel it for you?

I recently started coaching Julian, a teenager who has been anxious every morning before going to school. He would hardly speak over breakfast, thinking of what lay ahead, and then he'd have butterflies and break out in a sweat on his way to the school gate. He reported his level of anxiety was an 8 or 9 out of 10. I asked him what his challenge was. It was, in fact, a belief. "I can't relax on the mornings I have school." The tension in his voice was palpable. I asked him to add the word "yet" and see if anything changed.

He said it out loud. "I can't relax—yet—on the mornings I have school."

"And how does that make you feel?" I asked.

"I feel like there's hope" was the answer. My eyes almost teared up with joy. I knew his mom was extremely worried about him and that he had already seen a therapist for this, and nothing had changed.

After combining certain techniques from the following chapters, Julian has "become happier with who he is," is more relaxed going to school in the mornings, feels more comfortable in class, and has become more sociable with his classmates.

Silence your inner critic by flipping it

Although it's somewhat obvious, I recently learned on a deeper level that when you're looking to become healthier, it's not enough to put the good stuff in. You also must stop putting the bad stuff in, you know, the junk. You can eat five or more fruits and vegetables per day, but if you continue to binge regularly on chocolate, potato chips, soda, alcohol, and general junk food, you may never achieve your health goal. In a similar manner, when in the process of changing your limiting beliefs, you need to not only put in the new belief, but you also need to stop reinforcing harmful beliefs, such as...

- ☐ "I can never express myself well in meetings."
- ☐ "I'm useless with math."
- ☐ "I could never do what you do."
- ☐ "I'm too shy to ever say / ask ..."
- ☐ "I can never be assertive."

One of the things that frustrates me is hearing people speak like this about themselves aloud. What is that doing to the belief? It reinforces it even more. Most of us are guilty of this, myself included, but it's the mind's equivalent of junk food. but nonetheless, it's harmful. What do you think it does to your self-image? It puts it on its knees!

So, if or when you criticize yourself like this, firstly, bring it into your awareness. Then, once you're aware of it, flip it. Flip it there and then by asking yourself a question that will prove the self-critical thought untrue next time it comes up.

After thinking or saying, "I'm too shy to really say what I think or want," ask yourself, "What's one thing I can do to speak up a little more than I normally do?" When you catch yourself saying, "I'm always late for my appointments," then ask yourself, "How can I ensure I'm on time for my next appointment?" Then use the answer to take action to flip it, and guess what? That action is proof that your limiting belief is false. When you do speak up next, or you are on time, add it to your list on step 4 and repeat steps 5 and 6 above. Use that to further reinforce your new belief that you do speak up when you wish, or that you are someone who is on time for their appointments. Step by step, you're disproving these harmful beliefs.

By the way, our inner critic tends to use generalizations a lot. This can be a good thing, as it makes it easier to break those types of beliefs. You arrive at your next few appointments on time, and you can no longer believe "I'm always late for my appointments." You've just proven the opposite. Keep building up evidence to the contrary, and you build a more solid foundation for believing "I arrive on time for my appointments."

Your inner critic is also your friend

Your inner critic does have a useful purpose in small doses. It can highlight things that didn't go well so that you know you have something to work on and improve. For example, if you speak to your partner in a way that isn't very nice, then your inner critic can highlight this and bring it to your awareness. This can open up the possibility for you to apologize and speak better to them in the future. So, in small doses, and in certain contexts, it can be a good thing. We just want to ensure that when it goes over the line and becomes detrimental that we realize it and can flip it.

How do you want your life to be going forward? Identify the limiting beliefs that are holding you back from the life you desire and work on turning them around. Today's beliefs create your tomorrow...

CHAPTER 3

Give Yourself More "Likes"

"Plant seeds vs weeds."
— Jay Shetty

Imagine for a moment that you have twice the self-esteem and confidence in your abilities. What will you do with it? How would you handle your personal challenge? What or whom would you no longer accept in your life? How would it impact your career or relationships? What would it do for the quality of your life?

Let's focus on how we can boost both your confidence and self-esteem. First, let's look at how we act, and how we pull ourselves in the opposite direction.

A couple of years ago, I designed the content for a program on boosting one's resilience for a global multinational organization. The organization cares for the wellbeing of its associates, and among other initiatives, rolled out this 10-week program and associated webinars for its staff. I was leading a virtual session that focused on increasing self-esteem and asked a question to participants.

"Are we better at criticizing ourselves or complementing ourselves?'

I waited for the answers to come in on the MS Teams chat. On the other side of the camera were highly educated professionals with an average school level I estimate at master's degrees.

The answers flowed in…

- ☐ "Criticize."
- ☐ "Better at criticizing."
- ☐ "80 percent criticize."

Some of these professionals are the best in the world at what they do, and they're still better at putting themselves down than boosting themselves. Regardless of where I ask this question, regardless of the audience, regardless of their culture or age, the answers are similar.

Most of us are far better at criticizing and doubting ourselves than we are at complimenting ourselves, and we also do it more often. I don't necessarily mean out loud, but in our minds, where we have a constant flow of thoughts each day.

Let's see if any of these criticisms sound familiar to you…

- ☐ "I look old / fat / ugly…"
- ☐ "I'll never be comfortable speaking in public."
- ☐ "No wonder he / she left me."
- ☐ "I'll never be good at…"
- ☐ "I'm so stupid."
- ☐ "I always forget things."
- ☐ "I'm so unorganized."
- ☐ "I'm not good enough / young enough / intelligent enough / old enough / experienced enough / sexy enough / interesting enough…"

We all have our own favorites, of course, that we play over and over in our minds. Next question to each audience was: "What do you feel is the impact on your life?"

- ☐ "It lowers my self-esteem."
- ☐ "It drops my level of confidence in what I feel I'm capable of."

- [ ] "It holds me back from getting to the next level in my career."
- [ ] "It's resulted in me settling for someone who hasn't been very nice to me."

And the list goes on.

This incredible impact can at least be partly explained by the following.

A 2020 study carried out by psychologists at Queen's University in Canada has shown that we think on average 6,200 thoughts per day. Incredible, right?

Next question. Who do you think appears most often in your thoughts? Yes, you guessed it. You. Put your thoughts on a graph, and you show up way more often than anyone else there.

Now let's combine the fact that we think more than 6,000 thoughts in a day and most of them are about ourselves, and add the fact that most of those are negative thoughts that criticize us or doubt our abilities. Imagine what that's doing to our self-esteem.

The lens through which we see ourselves and the associated self-talk has extraordinary power. It can give us the leverage to unleash the incredible potential that each of us possess within. It can also do the opposite and hold us within certain self-imposed limits. What I'd like for you is to shatter these self-imposed limits and see the incredible potential that is yours.

How can you flip it around and at least achieve a better balance between your self-critic and becoming your own number one fan? Yes, fan is a strong word, and I'm using it here on purpose.

Firstly, let me say that being a fan of yourself is a good thing. You are the only one with you 24/7, so it's best that you like yourself, wouldn't you say? A true fan cheers on the team and shouts words of encouragement. When their star or team wins, they celebrate! And when they lose, after possibly voicing an expletive or two out of frustration, they voice words of encouragement, even if it's just aimed at the TV screen. Some also highlight what the star or team did well and try to understand what they should change to get a better result next time.

How about doing that for yourself? You do something well, you celebrate. You're not having a good day, or you didn't get the result you wanted, you give yourself words of encouragement and offer yourself ideas of what to do differently next time to get a better result.

Let's put it in social media terminology, shall we? How often do you give yourself a "Like" for being who you are or doing what you do?

Lots of us put "Likes" on things like the chocolate cake a friend made and posted on Facebook or on a photo on Instagram of someone sitting on a beach. So why not give yourself a "Like," either out loud or internally, for you being such an attentive partner today, or for stepping in to help the team, or for being such a kind person with a beautiful heart?

This isn't about being arrogant or pretentious. It's about getting yourself to a place where you are more aware of your qualities as a person, both on a conscious and subconscious level. We are aiming for a healthy balance and a way to boost your self-esteem.

Our self-talk can work with us and enable us to go for certain things or try to pull us back and protect us. In most cases, we want it to work with us, unless, of course, there is a real risk in doing so.

With higher self-esteem, you're better positioned to bounce back after a tough day, after someone leaves you, or if you lose your job. With higher self-esteem, you'll stop holding yourself back and instead, release more of your unique potential.

Focus on your qualities and strengths

I want you to make a list of what you like about yourself—your Wow List. This exercise isn't about saying you're so great at everything, that you're perfect as you are and that any employer or partner is so lucky to have you, and that you don't need to improve anything.

We can all strive to be better, to grow, and to continuously work on creating an even better version of ourselves. There is so much choice in the world today, both on a professional level and personal level, that we cannot stagnate. Continuing to strive to be better is what human beings excel at. However, this doesn't mean that we should not already accept and like who we are. We definitely should, so here it goes…

Create Your Wow List

Let's do this one in steps.

First, read the steps, and then jump right into the activity.

Step 1:
Go to a room or place that you can dance around like no one's watching. If there is someone there with you, why not dance around together, suggest they do this exercise with you, and then have fun comparing notes?

Step 2:
Pull out a pen and your journal or use the space below to write on.

Step 3:
Play your favorite energizing song on your phone or music app nice and loud and dance or jump around in whatever way you feel like moving. If you feel like singing out loud to it, be my guest.

Step 4:
Now that your energy is up and you feel invigorated, sit down, keep the music on if you wish, and write down all the things you like about yourself below.

That means list all your qualities, strengths, what you're good at, what your friends like about you, what your mother likes about you, what your boss likes about you... This is NOT the time to be humble. This is the time to be proud of who you are as a person.

Start your WOW List below (I'll start you off with a couple of examples).

What I like / love / appreciate about myself:

- ☐ I take care of my health.
- ☐ I love volunteering to help others or my community.
- ☐ I continue to learn and push myself.
- ☐ I look good in jeans.
- ☐ I contribute actively to my team.

In the space below, or in your journal, capture your WOW List

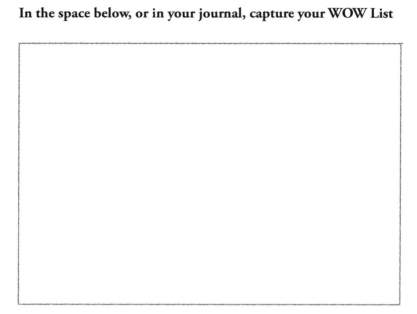

Step 5:

Now, stand up and say something to the effect of, "This is me, unique, beautiful, accepting of my flaws, and I freakin' rock!"

I suggest that next you rewrite your positive qualities on a card and put it somewhere visible, or at least where you can access it easily. Possibly on your mirror, on your bedside table, on the fridge, or wherever suits you best. It may not be something you want visible to your friends or family, but then again, why not? Wouldn't it be a great conversation starter with them, about what you appreciate about each other? What's important is that you read it regularly, hence one more step.

Step 6:

For at least the week ahead, look at the list every evening before you go to sleep and first thing in the morning when you wake.

In both cases, you can use a trigger for you to create this habit. In the first instance, getting into bed can be your trigger to review your list. In the second instance, the moment your feet touch the ground in the morning can act as your morning trigger.

Then, during or after each time you review your list, do something to enhance the good feeling. Smile in the mirror, or say "Yes," or repeat a powerful affirmation. Do something that will make you feel good. This will give you a pleasurable dopamine hit, and your brain will work with you in triggering you to do it more often.

These trigger moments or prompts are just suggestions, so please feel free to use whatever works for your situation and your personality.*

Bring it inside...internalize it!

Our subconscious works in images, so let's put your Wow List in there and reinforce it. It's quite simple, actually, and putting this list into your subconscious will help you reap the maximum benefit.

The subconscious is most open to suggestion when your brain is in alpha state or, quite simply, when you are between being fully awake and being asleep. We can put ourselves in a relaxed, meditative state for this, or instead use the moments just before we nod off to sleep or the moment when we just wake up. My preferred time and place for this activity is on my exercise mat at the end of a fitness session at home. I sit in a cross-legged posture, close my eyes, and calm my breath.

Find when and where works best for you and your lifestyle. Sit comfortably while taking in the silence and calming your mind. In this relaxed state, instead of reading your list, I want you to "see" yourself having each of those qualities you wrote down, one by one. This helps add or emphasize these in your self-identity, into who you believe you are as a person. As we act in accordance to how we believe we are, this reinforces those behaviors, and we start to see ourselves in a more positive light.

A couple of years back, I facilitated a workshop for leaders in an organization, where I walked them through a guided version of this exercise and they internalized their best qualities as a person, as we've just done here.

Right after, during a coffee break, one of the managers came to me and said he found the exercise both interesting and engaging and went on to share a personal story with me.

He said he used to be a musician, like most of his family, in fact, but hadn't touched an instrument in years. He lost interest due to a family fallout, of which I didn't seek any further details. I understood that it was something intense emotionally, and it caused him to have a negative connotation with playing music again. During the exercise, he saw himself as the musician that he was again, despite having a mental block around playing music. It was evident both from his words and his facial expressions that he found this rather surprising.

During lunch the next day, he purposely came and sat with me. It was clear he had something to share. After the usual courteous greetings and polite questioning about the morning session, he said, "You'll never guess what I did last night." Not knowing him prior to the event, I agreed. I had no idea. Had a beer? Discussed the workshop details with his wife? Nope.

"I took out my guitar and played it for the first time in years. I still don't understand how or why, as I had not planned it at all. It was like I was driven to it without thinking."

Part of his identity, which he confirmed during this guided internalization exercise that focused on his qualities, was that he is a great musician. He then just acted in accordance with who he was, without even consciously thinking about it or planning it.

Add something new to your list

While doing the same exercise, seeing your qualities, add on one character trait or quality that you would like to have and see yourself as having it already.

One day, during my internalization practice, I saw myself as a healthy eater. I clearly saw myself eating and relishing natural foods—raw carrot, apple, salads with fish, and drinking sparkling water with lemon. I focused on the sensation of feeling agile and dynamic with my body being more toned. It was a way of being, feeling, and living that I wanted more of, as my diet was too high in sweet snacks. I clearly remember the following day when I opened the fridge for a mid-afternoon snack. This would normally have been a piece of chocolate for my somewhat sweet tooth. That day was different. To my surprise, I had reached in and instead grabbed an apple. This was not a conscious decision but a subconscious one. As I was closing the fridge door, it felt like my conscious brain copped on to what I had just chosen, and I remember thinking, *No, never. An apple?* It was the visualization that triggered this new healthier behavior, and the apple was delicious, by the way.

This is incredibly powerful. Decide on that one thing you want to be more of, and then just include it in your internalization practice!

Now that you're more conscious of your qualities, take notice of small changes in your behavior and changes in your self-talk. A week or two from now, take a moment and check in with yourself. How are you feeling? What are you noticing that's different, related to what you've been internalizing? What impact has it had on you?

Your Compliments Diary

When you receive a compliment from someone, it feels good for a moment, and maybe, just maybe, a couple of weeks later, you still remember what they said. When you doubt yourself and your internal self-talk is negative, something you can equip yourself with to counterbalance this is the compliments you've received from others. Even if internal validation counts more for you than validation from others, these compliments can reinforce elements of your positive self-image when you need it most.

Below, or in your journal, capture the last compliment or positive feedback you received.

My last memorable compliment is...

It was from...

How this makes me feel is...

I encourage you to start to capture all of the compliments you receive in what I call a Compliments Diary, which, may be a section of your journal dedicated for this purpose.

P. S. This can also serve as a reminder to offer compliments to others and give them something more valuable and memorable than a "Like."

Your Victory List

Have you ever given much thought to what you have done, become, or achieved in your life that you can be proud about? Creating a Victory List offers you the chance to give yourself more "Likes" and boost your self-esteem. It'll help you to realize what you have done and how far you've come. It may also trigger the realization that you've achieved things in your life that at one point you thought were not possible for you, but you achieved them, regardless.

The list can include anything you are proud of, such as passing your driving test on the third attempt, losing 10 kilos and maintaining your new weight, having a loving, passionate relationship with your partner, achieving a specific role or level in your career, raising beautiful, caring children, speaking a second or third language fluently…

For each item on the list, add comments as to what makes you proud about that moment, specifically.

Give yourself the gift of this now. I invite you to get started in the table below, or in your journal.

What I'm proud of achieving, doing, becoming	I feel proud of this because …
Working and managing teams in a second language (French)	I barely scraped by in my school French exams, and no one would ever have believed I would speak French, let alone be managing a team of professionals in France, in their native tongue.

I encourage you to keep adding to your list as you remember your achievements, however big or bigger they may be. (There are no small achievements if you had to surpass yourself to get there.)

What does this list tell me about my potential, about what I am capable of becoming, having, or achieving in my life?

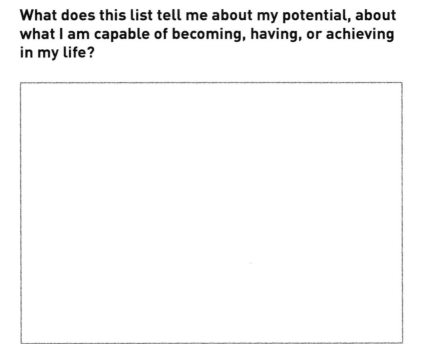

Reflect on your answer above and how you can apply this to your personal challenge or goal.

I'm sitting here writing this and wondering who would appreciate you sharing your list with them. How about pausing here for a moment to reflect? How would you feel sharing your Victory List with your partner, your child, your parents, or a close friend? How would they feel? Would it bring you closer and strengthen your bond? Would you feel embarrassed, and if so, why?

The key is to do it in a way that's humble and to not come across as pretentious. It could go something like… "I was just thinking of some things I'm proud of achieving in my life up to now. It was prompted by this book I read. The author calls it a Victory List. I realized that I had been focusing a lot on what I'm not good at and things I didn't do well. The exercise gave me a boost I needed and made me realize that I have done things in my life that I'm proud of. It's not even about what I achieved but rather how the achievements make me feel and the message that it sends about what each of us is capable of. Can I share an example of something 'small' I did and how that made me feel? I'd love to hear one of yours, how it makes you feel, and what it tells you about what you'd like to do more of going forward."

The decision is, of course, totally yours. If you are hesitating, then before deciding, I urge you to consider what they would get from it. If it would inspire them or bring you closer, I encourage you to do it. If not, or if you believe it to be inappropriate, then maybe let it be for now. Do whatever feels right for you.

Activity: Daily Wins

For the next 10 days, select a moment at the end of each day to write down what you did well that day. Take note of your daily wins and see what that does for your self-esteem.

I leave you with this…

You can never outperform your own self-image. It's yours for the making, so make it an incredible one!

* For a more details on how to create such habits, check out Tiny Habits from BJ Fogg

CHAPTER 4

Get in the Zone in 2 Minutes!

"The mind is everything. What you think, you become."
— Buddha

It was my early morning drive for another typical day at the office. On a good day, without any traffic incidents, it took an hour of focused driving to arrive on time. Exactly one hour from the moment I shut the door of my thick, stone-walled, wooden-beamed house in Riquewihr, the most quaint and picturesque of villages on the Alsace Wine Road, up to the time I arrived at the door of our contemporary glass office building, designed by a Canadian architect.

Every morning felt like a short time travel of a couple of hundred years from that medieval village to this innovation center sitting on the Rhine River that hosts some of the brightest scientific and business minds in the world.

Today I needed to be on time for my first meeting. It was an important one. It was with my manager, together with the department director, for a mid-year discussion on what I'd achieved compared to what was planned at the start of the year. The conversation would cover what went well during the first six months of the business year, what I was most proud of achieving, how I'd been leveraging my strengths, and what they both could do to help for the last two quarters of the year. All quite standard in such an organization.

My department director is very strategic. He was brought in to create this new central learning organization, get buy-in from our stakeholders, establish the initial high-level objectives of the team, and build our brand reputation.

At that point in my career, being strategic was not one of my strengths. It was something I needed to develop. I was functioning more on an operational level to establish a world-class learning portfolio to train associates globally. To connect with him and be seen in a good light, I needed the discussion to be strategic, rather than discussing operational details.

During my drive, I reflected on this dilemma. I quieted the music from my playlist and reflected on the outcome I wanted.

I wanted him to be impressed by my ability to analyze and communicate on strategy, and therefore be sure that I was still the right person for this key role on the team.

OK, *so how do I need to be to get this outcome?*

I can't control how it will go and cannot determine how my manager and director will act, but I can control how I will be. At least if I'm relaxed and confident, that is.

Hmmmm, I thought, *how DO I need to be?*

Let's see… Confident, listen to understand, think strategically, and speak clearly at a relaxed pace. Yes, that's exactly how I need to be.

I arrived at a parking space, turned off the ignition, and ran through a two-minute exercise I call a Rapid Effective Preparation, or simply a REP.

It's an incredibly effective and fast technique to get yourself to show up in a way that best matches how you need to be in order to achieve the outcome you're aiming for. You set your intentions in advance as to how you want to act based on the outcome you desire, and you step into this behavior in your mind.

You can use it before a presentation, a meeting, a date, a competition, an exam or even just before you see your family at the end of your day's work.

This is how it works...

Step 1:
Decide on the outcome you are looking to achieve.

Step 2:
Put yourself in a strong posture by sitting or standing upright, head up, eyes forward, and breathing from your belly (more on this later in the chapter).

Step 3:
Ask yourself how you need to be to achieve your desired outcome. I suggest a max of 3 to 4 behaviors or traits (speak with high energy, be confident, listen with empathy...or whatever your desired outcome for the event calls for you to be).

Step 4:
Focus and tell yourself this is how you are now, and each time you say how you are, you see yourself being that way and feel how that feels inside.

Step 5:
Do something to celebrate and give your brain a sort of dopamine hit (smile, clap your hands together, say, "Yes," etc.).

Here is how I did a REP for my meeting with the director:

Step 1:
I decided on the outcome I wanted...to show the director that I could be strategic in my thinking and that I continued to be the right person for the role.

Step 2:
I sat up straight, with a strong posture, in the car.

Step 3:
For my desired outcome, I decided that I needed to be confident, listen to understand, and think and speak strategically.

Step 4:
One by one, I went through how I needed to be to achieve the outcome I wanted. I said, in a medium-pitched voice, "I'm confident." At the same time, I saw myself being confident, and I aligned my physiology to that of being confident. I went in my mind to a recent moment where I felt really confident and in the zone for a similar situation and homed in on that image and feeling. In this case, it was speaking up in a meeting where I was describing a solution to a challenge we had on the team. I locked onto that feeling of confidence I had at that moment and felt it again.

Next was "I listen to understand," and I saw myself listening intently and absorbing what was being said.

Then, "I think and speak strategically," seeing myself thinking at a high level and making strategy suggestions that would add value to our team's work while taking my time to find my wording.

Step 5:
I finished off by tapping one hand with the other while saying "Yes" to myself. To really compliment these affirmations in Step 4, I add a specific gesture of my hand for each one. I find that integrating my body into the activity somehow really enforces it and gives it more power.

With my right hand raised to eye level, I make purposeful gestures, with my hand making almost a 90-degree angle, starting above eye level and working down, one by one, for each affirmation.

When using your hands with your body, feel free to experiment with what works for you until you find your specific technique.

*To see this in action, check out the short video on my website www.trevorlynch.net

Back to my meeting. I find these reviews somewhat intense and therefore a little stressful. Around halfway through, I was answering one of the strategic questions and I was surprised at how well it was going.

I was listening to understand, and pausing, before replying with a strategic response in a calm, confident tone.

I mentally stepped back from myself at this point and thought, *This freakin' works!! Incredible!*

The ultimate confirmation came 10 minutes before the end, when before having to leave a few minutes early, the director said, "Before going, I have one last question. What did you change or do differently this time, as I find you very different to last time, in a positive way?"

Hmmm, will I tell him about this process?

Nah, I chose not to, and gave another more "reasonable" explanation.

Where to REP it?

You may be wondering where can you do the REP exercise and not look or sound silly? Good question.

I normally do this in a place where I won't be disturbed, or at least not have people around me. If I am in a hotel before a live workshop, it's the last thing I do before leaving my room, and I do it standing in front of a mirror, full or half-length if possible.

If I am driving to the office (just like the example in the beginning of this chapter), I REP in my car, eyes open, obviously, and I minimize the hand gestures, of course, or I do it where I can pull in safely for a few minutes.

Another common place I've practiced this, just before a meeting or delivering a workshop, is in the men's room. Yes, permission to giggle at the thought of that, no worries. In that case, I don't speak aloud, of course:-) Depending on where the event is, and depending what time of day it's happening, this is often the only option.

So, it's completely up to you to find what location would work best for your particular challenge or goal and take two minutes to do this. With a little practice, that's literally how long it will take, two minutes!

REP dos and don'ts

Can you find what was common between each of these steps?

Firstly, I see each behavior in my mind. I don't just say the words. I didn't just say "I'm confident" and "I listen to understand." I saw myself being that way each time. Since the subconscious works with images and not words, and it controls 95 percent of what we do and how we do it, that's the part I aim to reach with this. Affirmations of wanted behaviors can be very powerful by themselves, though I find adding this imagery more powerful again.

What else did you notice?

I focused on me and not on those I was interacting with. As we cannot control other people's behavior, it's best to focus on our own behavior, which can and most often does have an impact on how others respond. Each phrase starts with "I" and is said in the present tense. "I am…" "I listen…" Whenever we use the word "I," our brain sits up and pays attention, especially when we speak about ourselves in the present tense. It's like a message to the subconscious that says, "This must be important, so I need to focus."

In addition, when we use the present tense, it's like a super-urgent message to the brain. So instead of saying "I will be confident," say "I am confident." In other words, "This is how I am right now; take me to that behavior or way of being now." If we use future language, then the brain doesn't have to worry about it so much and goes back to what's important in the present moment.

There's one more thing. Each step focused on what I want, not on what I want to avoid! This is key! The brain doesn't (always) hear the negative.

Let me demonstrate this to you. Repeat the following sentence to yourself several times.

"I don't feel stressed."

"I don't feel stressed."

"I don't feel stressed."

What message is your brain hearing? What is the keyword or keywords here?

"Feeling stressed," right? When you repeat it, especially during a stressful moment, focus on any changes inside of you. Does it leave you more or less stressed than before you repeated it? We know now that the subconscious works with images, so the image it's picking up on is that you're stressed, so saying this to yourself internally may actually make you feel this way! I divert for a moment from this example and ask you not to think of how melting chocolate tastes in your mouth. Don't think of the sweet, creamy taste and velvety texture of the chocolate melting. Just emphasizing the point above.

Always transform a negative expression into its positive equivalent, so here we could replace "I don't feel stressed" with "I feel confident" or "I'm feeling incredibly relaxed." Feel how that is interpreted by your body in comparison to "not feeling stressed."

As I said before, you may be OK taking your chances and doing things the way you've always done them, and that's perfectly fine, at least for some events.

The thing is, if you want to maximize your possibility of getting the results that you're seeking, then how about doing something new for two minutes beforehand, like the REP exercise?

Use it to prepare for some aspect of the personal challenge you identified for yourself in Chapter 1. If your personal challenge is being a better spouse or parent for example, you could do a REP just before you see them at the end of your day's work to get yourself in a state of being calm, present, curious about their day, and being complimentary towards them.

You are helping your brain work with you so you have the best chance of getting the result you're aiming for.

One last thing. I mentioned being in a strong physiology or posture before starting with your REP. Put yourself into the physiology or posture that you're normally in when you're feeling in the zone. A posture in which you feel strong and confident. A posture that reminds you of a moment when all was going well, when you were performing in exactly the way you needed to, making the impact that you were looking to make. Sit or stand straight, your feet grounded on the floor, your head upright. Breathe deeply, inhaling through your nose.

Activity: Anchor Your Confident State

If you're in an environment where you can safely close your eyes and not be disturbed, then I invite you to do this next exercise after you read the steps below.

Sit in a posture that's comfortable and strong, then close your eyes. For a couple of minutes, just bring your focus to your breath.

Then, when you're feeling relaxed, I want you to go back to a time where you felt incredibly confident, preferably, but not necessarily, in a context similar to your upcoming challenge. The key here is that you were feeling incredibly confident. It's the you that was making it happen, whatever the "it" was at the time.

Now, hold onto that moment and go back into your body as you were then. Feel how you felt. Stand how you stood or sit as you were sitting then. Say what you were saying to yourself then. Put on that same facial expression as you did when you were feeling incredibly confident.

Yes. That's it. Now, hold that feeling and zoom into it. Double its intensity, making it stronger, boosting your confidence even further. Right now, at about the peak of this feeling, squeeze your thumb and forefinger together. Give yourself a powerful affirmation. Nod your head and smile. Then come back to focusing on your breath for a couple of minutes. You're feeling strong. You're feeling confident. You're feeling unstoppable. Then, move your fingers and toes and come back to the present moment.

For a guided version of this, visit my resources page at www. trevorlynch.net or use the QR code below.

Repeat this every day for a week or so, more if you wish. In addition, each time you feel really confident going forward, when you feel the peak of confidence, squeeze the same thumb and forefinger together.

This is known as an anchor, and when you then repeat this gesture in other situations, it will help you feel that confidence when you need it.

Any time you feel a strong emotion, your brain is looking to see what caused it. As you've repeated this several times, what was common when you felt confident was that you had that thumb and forefinger squeezed together. Then, at a later date, when you squeeze them together in that same way, your brain takes this as a message that now you're feeling confident and takes you to a similar state of confidence.

The next time you do a REP and want to connect to a feeling of being confident, sit or stand tall and strong and as you tell yourself that you're confident, squeeze that same thumb and forefinger together to recreate that feeling inside of you.

For your personal challenge, add a short REP beforehand, reinforce it as needed with a strong anchor, and you will be astounded by how you show up.

CHAPTER 5

Visualization Part I ...
How & Why You Should
Absolutely Do This

"Victorious warriors win first and then go to war,
while defeated warriors go to war first and then seek to win."
— Sun Tzu, *The Art of War*

Chloe was awake half the night thinking about it. At 9:00 a.m., she would make a presentation to her company's senior management team. The reason for her being awake? At her last presentation a month ago, her voice was a little shaky, and the words didn't quite come out as she had planned. She wasn't convincing and she beat herself up afterwards. Right after the presentation, her manager asked if she was OK. Translation of what her manager said, at least in Chloe's mind, was: "What happened to you just now?"

The thing is, she knew her topic well for that last presentation and was as prepared as ever. So, what happened? The atmosphere at home had been quite tense with her partner, and on top of that, it felt like traffic had doubled that morning on her route to the office. For almost the full duration of her drive to work, she saw herself arriving late to the meeting, panting and flushed. She envisioned herself receiving disapproving looks from some members of her upcoming presentation audience, so her stress levels had skyrocketed even before she got to present.

This time, she found herself awake at 3:00 a.m., reviewing her slides one more time. All night, she saw how her upcoming presentation would go horribly wrong. Again.

This is visualization. "What?" I hear you wondering. "I thought visualization was a good thing, something top athletes and performers use to get better results, to up their game."

Yes, you'd be right. Visualization can be positive or negative.

The mind works with images and, if left to its own devices, may very well play images that are disempowering and create stress for you. It'll play back images of the past, of similar situations that may have happened years ago and often will highlight what went wrong. This is what happened to Chloe.

Our brain has a negativity bias, which means we tend to pay more attention to negative experiences than experiences that are positive, and we tend to remember them more. It's thought to be an adaptive evolutionary function. Earlier in human history, paying attention to bad, dangerous, and negative threats in the world was literally a matter of life and death. Those who were more attuned to danger and who paid more attention to the bad things around them were more likely to survive. To keep us safe, the brain highlights risks to help us avoid certain situations or events. Unless we consciously take control of the movie in our mind of how upcoming, challenging events may go, it may not be a nice movie to watch. Not such a happy ending. The key is to play the film we desire. To consciously write the script and play the role of the main character performing as we imagine in the key scenario.

In the above example, it wasn't lack of preparation that caused Chloe to struggle in her first presentation. It was her mind. Allowing her mind to play all those negative scenarios while driving, as if they were real, had boosted her critical self-talk and didn't allow her to get into the zone. Almost like she didn't have a chance to be her best when she really needed to be.

Let's swing it around and truly up her chances, and yours, of a successful outcome when we need it. To do that, we'll use what I call Targeted Visualization.

Let's start with understanding visualization.

You already practiced a short form of visualization in Chapter 4 in the form of a REP. Now we're going to take an in-depth look at the benefits and applications of visualization.

Research has shown that to our brains, there's little or no difference between a powerful visualization and the actual experience. But what is visualization?

Visualization is the ability to create pictures in your mind. Visualization is something you do every day. It's basically seeing with your mind, or playing a film in your mind like we all do on occasion. Actually, more than on occasion. We play films in our minds every day.

Think about it. If your partner is late arriving home, your mind starts to play images of what could have happened to them, where they are, and what it is they're doing that could explain why they didn't let you know when they would arrive. If you are the one who's late arriving somewhere, you're imagining how your host or colleagues will react when you get there. Before your team meeting, you may imagine how it'll go and how it will go on at least 10 minutes over like it usually does.

When you get up and you think about what you're going to do, do you just say the words, or do you see yourself doing it or having to do it?

Let's say you have a difficult conversation coming up over the phone. Before you pick up your phone, there's a strong possibility you'll imagine how it will go in advance. Even if it's just for an instant beforehand, chances are high that if you're finding it stressful, you'll play out at least part of how it may go, or how it may go wrong, in your mind.

Most of the time when we're visualizing, it's our subconscious mind playing on autopilot, instead of us taking control and playing the film we want, based on how we'd like events to go.

So, how about choosing now to take control of what you see in your mind to get you to the results that you want?

How it feels in the body

It's been proven that when you think about a stressful event, it creates the same biochemical reactions as you actually living that event. Try this for a moment. Think of an event that normally causes you stress or anxiety. It may be going to the dentist, having to speak in front of a few hundred people, a parachute jump out of a plane, an argument with your boss, or whatever it is for you. Think about who's around you, what's going on, how are you standing, sitting, or moving. Think about what you're hearing, what people are saying, what you're saying, and how you're saying it. Now close your eyes and see yourself vividly in that moment. Immerse yourself in the context and observe what's happening in your body.

Does your heart rate speed up or slow down? Does anything feel tight? Are your facial muscles more tense or more relaxed? Is there stress or anxiety manifesting itself in your body?

Let's flip it now and get to a nice place. I'd like you to imagine you're lying on a sandy beach. You're lying on a towel, and your right hand is touching the fine sand. You rub some grains of sand between your thumb and fingertips. You feel the sun's rays warming your bare skin. You hear the flow of the ocean, it's waves gently rolling over as they arrive at the water's edge. Your nose detects the fragrance of sun cream wafting through the air. You open your eyes from behind your sunglasses to marvel at this beautiful day under a virgin blue sky. Again, close your eyes and really step into that moment.

Now, before you rush off and book a weekend at the coast, allow me to ask you a few questions, if I may. How did that feel? Different to the previous experience, right?! What happened? You're just sitting there, reading this book. You haven't gone anywhere or done anything. Why did you feel different this time? You didn't just go through a stressful situation, and you're most probably not yet lying on that beach.

In the first example, your body did not react to a stressful event; it reacted to you imagining yourself being in that stressful event. In the second example, you didn't feel relaxed and chilled out because you were lying on a beach; you did so only because you imagined yourself there. And not just imagined, but imagined vividly. You imagined it so vividly that your mind felt it to be true on some level and created the associated bodily sensations.

Interesting concept. So how can we use this to trick our minds into believing that something has already happened? And how will that serve us?

Why might you be nervous speaking in public, visiting the dentist, or going on a first date? It's because a part of your brain senses that this is uncomfortable for you. Your brain wants to keep you away from risk and pain and so plays images of the event in advance in an attempt to persuade you to avoid it. It basically wants to keep you safe.

If your brain believes that you've done this already, and it went well, and was even pleasurable, then this guard goes down or at least relaxes somewhat. Guess what that does. It lowers your level of nervous anticipation and anxiety that you normally relate to the event.

How can you do that? By vividly visualizing the event going as you want it to go and seeing you being how you need to be in order to make it so. When you see yourself already having accomplished your goal, it becomes integrated into your brain as part of your self-image, and then your brain works with you in that direction, instead of holding you back.

What is Targeted Visualization, and how can I use it?

Targeted Visualization is the act of using the power of your imagination to create vivid, believable future conditions for some upcoming challenge in your life. You step into that future moment and see it as if it's already happened. You were exactly as you needed to be in order to get the result you were aiming for.

Visualization techniques can often be referred to as creative visualization. Creative visualization can help you achieve ambitious goals like a dream house or sports car. It creates what's known as cognitive dissonance in your brain. Your brain acknowledges that there is a difference between what you are seeing to be true in your life and what is actually the case. It then pulls you forward to fill the gap between your current circumstances and what you have vividly imagined to be true.

Although creative in nature, I prefer to call the version in this book "Targeted Visualization." We're using it to be at our best for specific events or challenges, or to be better than what we believed ourselves capable of up to now, rather than to manifest certain monetary or material outcomes. Using Targeted Visualization, we will focus on specific outcomes for your personal challenge or upcoming events that are important for you.

A word of caution here is that for most events, visualization alone will not be sufficient. Creatively visualizing yourself winning the lottery or sitting on your luxury yacht in Saint Tropez will not realize that dream for you by itself. You still need to put the work in to get there. In a similar way, Targeted Visualization will influence the outcome of your upcoming event or challenge in the direction you desire and is complementary to any preparation you do. It doesn't replace your preparation but is an extremely effective addition to your prep work.

If you put the work in and then complement it with Targeted Visualization, it can make an incredible difference to your level of performance.

The benefits of using visualization

Lindsey Vonn, one of the most successful female skiers in history, said in an interview, "I always visualize the run before I do it. By the time I get to the start gate, I've run that race 100 times already in my head, picturing how I'll take the turns."

But she doesn't just keep the images in her head. She's also known to include physically simulating the path by literally shifting her weight back and forth as if she were on skis, as well as practicing the specific breathing patterns she'll use during the race. She brings it to a higher level by physically moving her body in similar ways to how she aims to move in her actual race. Such a wonderful example of Targeted Visualization in practice.

Visualization has the effect of making your subconscious believe on a certain level that what you want to achieve has already happened, which, in turn, does several things.

- ☐ It helps you to be more relaxed and excited about an upcoming challenge or goal.
- ☐ It increases the chances of you acting as you visualized in your mind.
- ☐ It helps release your potential.
- ☐ It reduces your self-doubt and enforces your self-confidence.
- ☐ It helps engrain new habits, as neural pathways in the brain that are created by performing an activity are also created just by visualizing yourself performing the activity.

How to visualize effectively

When starting with visualization, it is important to relax. As I mentioned previously, when the body and mind are deeply relaxed, we enter into what's known as the alpha brain state. It is in this state that your subconscious is more open to the images you consciously play. Here's one way to do it:

- ☐ Sit somewhere you can be calm and not be disturbed.
- ☐ Create a clear idea of what it is you want to do or achieve.
- ☐ Take deep breaths and exhale slowly, close your eyes, and relax into a deep, calm, meditative state of mind.
- ☐ From that relaxed state, see yourself in the environment you'll be in for your challenge. Step into yourself and feel how it feels to perfectly do what you want to do and to be

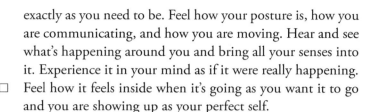

exactly as you need to be. Feel how your posture is, how you are communicating, and how you are moving. Hear and see what's happening around you and bring all your senses into it. Experience it in your mind as if it were really happening.

☐ Feel how it feels inside when it's going as you want it to go and you are showing up as your perfect self.

☐ Repeat it as often as you feel necessary, depending on your desired outcome, what's at stake, and how much you really want it.

When you visualize, depending on the event, make it as real as possible. If you see yourself running a race, then you could see what you would see on your route, hear your footsteps treading the ground, feel the sun caressing your face, and feel the fluidity and lightness of your body, seeing yourself run past other competitors as you reach the finish line. You could continue and see yourself celebrating your new fastest time with friends, while feeling relaxed and proud of your achievement.

Something I love about visualization is that it only takes a few minutes and can be done from anywhere. Let me go back on that; it can take even less.

If you've seen an international rugby match, notice what the kicker does when aiming to score a penalty kick. I have Ireland's highest-point scorer in mind here, Ronan O' Gara. Before every penalty kick or conversion, he steps back from the ball in a set sequence, and then, before kicking, he looks up at the posts, visualizes the ball going between them, and then kicks. A few short seconds right in the middle of a match that can help make the difference to the outcome.

That brings me to the question of where to visualize. I've done it in my car parked up in a highway gas station for 10 minutes, while sitting on my sofa, from a lotus-type position on my mat after exercising, and on a train with a headset on to minimize distractions. You get to do this from wherever is suitable for you, your schedule, and your lifestyle.

Depending on where I am at the time, I may play a relaxing piece of music or just sit in silence. Both work well, and I did find that when I first started practicing this technique, playing that same relaxing melody did help anchor it in and get me "in the zone" more easily. I suggest experimenting with both to find what works best for you.

I should add an important point here. Visualization cannot be used to control the behavior of others. It cannot determine if an interviewer will like you, what your competitor does, or if your first date will be charmed by your sense of humor. With this in mind, focus your visualization mainly on you and how *you* will show up, in order to maximize your chances of getting the outcome you desire.

Leverage your practice moments

The more often you practice what you want to improve or perfect, the easier it becomes and the more likely it is that you'll find yourself in the zone, with it going or flowing as you wish. It is important to practice for lower stakes events so that this feeling can then be more easily locked onto during your visualization practice when you may be feeling the pressure for your higher stakes event.

For most challenges, there are several ways to practice. One way is to do something similar in advance of the big event. For example, if your big event is a job interview for your dream job, then you could apply for other roles and interview for them in advance of your "big interview." I'm not suggesting wasting the interviewers' time, but to select roles that could potentially be interesting for you, even if they don't sound as interesting as your ideal job. With less at stake, you'll feel more relaxed and can later more easily tune into that same state of mind. Another preparation strategy is to role play with someone like a colleague, a coach, or a mentor until you feel more confident. It may feel a little strange to be interviewed by someone who knows you well, so ask them to play the role with questions prepped and give you honest feedback on what you did well and what to work on.

If it's a big presentation, you could volunteer to deliver presentations with less at stake for you or with a smaller or less intimidating audience. Again, less at stake means less pressure and a higher chance of you working from that best version of you.

Another possibility is to practice presenting out loud, not just silently in your mind. When you practice out loud, it's more real and starts to build the neural pathways associated with your presenting style. I've often voice- or video-recorded myself and played it back while positioning myself as an observer to see how I did. Hearing your own voice or seeing yourself on video may take some getting used to, but the insights make it worth the effort. If you are not happy with how you sounded or how you opened the presentation, you can always go back and do it again until you're happy with it. Lock in the feeling of you in the flow, performing well, and being proud of it.

Regardless of the challenge, when possible, never leave the scene of a practice session without feeling good about at least one aspect of your performance.

What we're aiming for here are several things. We're looking to build your confidence, as well as your skill and experience, and in preparation for your pre-challenge visualizations, enable you to more easily imagine feeling how you want to feel on the day. This will make it easier for your brain to lock on to the sensation of you being in the flow.

When you experience the flow, you can more readily visualize yourself in it, feel the sensation of confidence, and in addition, use that sensation when doing a REP just beforehand. You may, for example, decide that the behaviors you focus on for your REP include feeling confident, finding your words easily, and using deliberate pauses as you speak. By practicing these in advance, it's easier for you to then lock onto those feelings and REP them just before your real event.

During recent weeks, I delivered live workshops to approximately 3,000 participants virtually on subject areas such as being strong during challenging times and creating new habits. I would have broken out in a sweat if I had to do this when I was 10 years younger, so it's not a natural gift I have.

The way I prepared impacted how I felt my performance went, and I also experimented with it a little. As they were virtual events, I was in my house, sometimes standing, other times sitting. Before including a targeted visualization in my preparation, I practiced aloud in the exact location in my house that I would be during the real events. This had the most benefit. I spoke as if I was live in front of a virtual audience, stood and sat as I would be positioned on the day, and gestured with my hands as I normally do at certain moments.

Those of you who have given a presentation on Zoom or Microsoft Teams will understand this next piece. It can feel strange and uncomfortable to focus your eyes on the camera lens when you present, but if you don't do it, your audience may feel like you're not making eye contact with them. I find it essential to include this in my practice, as it's off-putting when having to do it in reality if you're not used to it.

Regardless of your challenge, the message here is to practice in conditions as similar as possible to the environment and context you'll encounter, so as to build your confidence in advance.

Tap into the power of visualization

Visualization means using the power of your imagination. If your imagination can make you feel stressed or joyful, just from what you are focusing it on, then it can also help you feel more confident. When you see and experience its power, and your ability to unleash potential that is within you, it'll become part of how you think and how you prepare yourself. For some, it's not easy to visualize. It takes focus and real conscious effort. For others, it comes more naturally. Remember what it was like learning to drive or to ride a bike? The more you do it, the more the conscious, focused effort becomes automatic. It's the same with visualization.

What would you attempt if you really believed that you could do it? What would your life be like? Think for a moment of what that would change for you. Visualization will help you get there and move you out of your comfort zone more easily and more often.

It'll help turn on that potential you have in a way you may not have experienced up to now.

Next, let's get practical with visualizations so you can utilize this technique when you really need it.

CHAPTER 6

Visualization Part II ... Perform When It Matters

"Stop being afraid of what can go wrong,
and start being excited about what can go right."
—Tony Robbins

Andy, a friend, had been preoccupied with his father's cancer diagnosis for several days. Perhaps, it was just his imagination playing games with him, but he was feeling tingling sensations in the same place where his father had his tumors. *Could this be genetic? Am I imagining it? How can I find out?* The questions went on and on in that direction as he was driving to his new girlfriend's place after work. All he could think of was: *What if I have that cancer too?*

He switched his mind to his romantic date. Despite the fact that it was a relatively new relationship, he had no sexual urge whatsoever at that moment. *It's not good to be thinking about this right now. It would be fine if I were heading home, but it's definitely not OK when I'm heading out on a date.*

How the hell is Mr. Happy going to stand up and play this evening, with this tremendous worry on the top of my mind?

He started to think of different possibilities. *Should I cancel and say I'm not feeling well? Is there something I should take?*

He arrived near her place, found a parking space, turned off the engine, and closed his eyes.

Who cares if a passerby finds this funny? If it works, it'll be worth it.

After about five minutes of visualizing how his intimate evening would go, he left the car and headed to her apartment.

What will happen with Andy's date? Will this work for something that seems to be as overwhelming as his immediate health concern and get him in that sexual energy zone?

All he told me was that the evening was beautiful, the sex was incredible, and he's still in great health.

When our minds are really preoccupied, or worried, Mr. Happy doesn't always stand to attention or Miss Happy doesn't always open up for the occasion. Let's say our sexual organs aren't demanding or receiving the attention they merit. They don't necessarily get the stimulation they desire. It's like the brain is saying, "Hey, don't be selfish. I need to focus on this other thing." This can come from a problem at work, worry about a serious health issue, conflicts in your relationship, and even first-date nerves. The good news is visualization can help.

Visualization practice for your personal challenge

I've used visualization, and continue to do so, to be more confident in meetings and job interviews, to eat healthier, to exercise more often, to give great presentations, to be more effective with getting the most important tasks done in a day, and also, like Andy, to boost my sex life. Where is it most useful for you right now? It may be the personal challenge you identified in Chapter 1, or it may be something else that you have on your mind that is causing you stress just thinking about it. Define what that is for you and continue with the activity below.

Read through the following, then, if you're in a comfortable and safe setting to do so, close your eyes and walk through the steps. You can also find the guided version at www.trevorlynch.net

Focus on your breath and relax for a minute or two.

Center your mind on your challenging opportunity.

Decide on what it is you want as the outcome, based on what's within your control. Be as specific as you can so your brain really gets what the target is.

See yourself in that moment, being the way you need to be and doing what you need to do in order to achieve your desired outcome. What are you seeing? What are you doing? What do you hear, taste or smell? Picture it all in vivid detail.

Step into yourself being and acting that way. As you do so, hold yourself in a confident posture and feel how it feels to be in the zone.

Visualize a challenge popping up and you handling it magnificently.

You may wish to nod your head as you do, give yourself a strong positive affirmation, and anchor in the confident feeling by squeezing your thumbs and the tips of your forefingers together.

Tell yourself, "From now on, I am confident in my ability and adaptability to do this (or any words to that effect that resonate with you)."

Open your eyes again and acknowledge yourself for a great visualization.

To give you a real example, this is me prepping for a live workshop using this targeted visualization.

I often do some form of physical activity first, such as yoga or a fitness session, to feel better in my body.

I sit cross-legged on my mat, close my eyes, and gently focus on my breath, which I make a little deeper and longer.

I bring my mind to the upcoming event, and I ask myself what outcome I want from it. This may be something like, "I want the participants to walk away feeling incredible about themselves, for them to go deep and make certain realizations about their capabilities, or for them to say this was the best live workshop or training they've had."

I then see myself in the flow and being how I need to be for that to happen.

I consciously sit tall on my mat, step into myself in my mind delivering the workshop, and feel myself performing in a way that enables the outcome I'm seeking.

I'm visualizing myself speaking authentically, responding empathetically to comments in the chat, allowing myself to show vulnerability, and using my voice to create a certain energy.

I often nod my head during parts of this, while silently telling myself, "Yes, I love doing this and I'm freakin' great at it."

I use an anchor when feeling at the peak of my confidence, where I squeeze the tips of my forefingers to the tips of my thumbs.

I use an affirmation before I finish that goes something like: "Whatever happens, I'll find a solution, and all will go well."

I come back to focusing on my breath one last time, open my eyes, and may say something like, "OK, I'm ready!"

If you find it challenging, here are some tips for you:

- ☐ Try it with relaxing music in the background.
- ☐ If it's hard to stay focused for the duration, then do it with your finger on the fast forward button of your film. See it happening as you desire, just speeded up.
- ☐ Go online and find images or videos of people doing what you want to do. This will help you to project yourself into that same situation and simulate what they're doing, but in your own way. Close your eyes and project yourself into this

video or image, acting and speaking in a similar manner to the role model you've just observed and studied.

☐ Participants at my workshops have often said that having a voice guide them from one step to the next makes all the difference. To get you kicked off in your practice, follow my guided visualizations at... www.trevorlynch.net

While visualization is an extremely powerful tool, which can yield incredible results, we have years of negative thought patterns built up that we need to balance out. In my life, I've seen results with it around 90 percent of the times I've used it. In most cases when I didn't get the result I was aiming for, there was another underlying cause, such as lack of preparation for the event, or I was unsure if what I was aiming for was something I really wanted, or I hadn't foreseen a challenge popping up that I would have to deal with.

To ensure best results, check in on if it's what you truly desire, prepare well for the technicalities of your event, and include dealing with an unexpected challenge in your visualization. See something go wrong and you managing it like a pro.

Experiment with visualization for various challenges and goals you have, at various times of the day, with and without music, guided or self-led, for any challenge for which you believe it will help you to be, and even surpass, what you currently believe is your best you.

Visualization for the bedroom

The bedroom can be such a delicate place emotionally. It can be a place of incredible connection and intimacy and can also be a source of apprehension or frustration. Couples do not always have the same desires at the same moment. One feels like sleeping, while the other is hoping for physical connection. One is feeling hopeful as they enter the bedroom; the other has a temporary feeling of hostility over an unresolved issue between them.

On top of that, there are days when, like Andy, you just have too much going on in your mind and are not feeling the desire.

Visualization can help you create a deeper bond and a more intense level of physical desire and connection.

One way to use visualization for the bedroom is to follow the steps below.

If it's well enough in advance of your possible intimate moment, starting at Step 1 may create a nice connection and anticipation. If you do this just before your possible intimate moment, go right to visualizing Step 2.

Step 1:

See yourself being affectionate and romantic to your partner, in advance of a possible more intimate connection. See yourself doing something nice for them, saying loving words, and setting a romantic tone. If they are near you, see yourself looking them in the eyes and kissing them on the mouth or cheek. Let them know you "see" them. Your focus is on them feeling appreciated and loved.

Step 2:

Fast forward to when you are together in the bedroom or to the place where you can be more intimate. See, feel, and taste your first kiss. See yourself getting more erotic, at a pace that you are sure will please your partner. Feel how that is in your body and see how your body is reacting to your partner. See the moment going exactly as you wish. See yourself pleasing, possibly surprising, your partner. Go right to the end of the scene and end it with you both in each other's arms.

Visualization will help you program your mind and body for what's coming up, but it won't do the same for your partner. If they are not in the mood for intimacy, be sure to respect them and how they feel and repeat your visualization on a day when both of you are more in phase.

Let's add in an affirmation or two

Affirmations are positive, powerful phrases or statements that can help you overcome self-sabotaging and negative thoughts. All you need to do is pick a phrase that resonates with you and repeat it to yourself. Affirmations can help replace negative self-talk narratives, boost your self-esteem, and motivate you.

A few rules to have them work for you...

☐ Start them in the present tense with "I."
☐ Say what you are, not what you are not.
☐ Keep them short so you can remember them easily and say them with conviction.
☐ Make them specific.

Here are some examples to help you get started. You have to feel a connection to the words in order for them to work for you, so decide on yours at your leisure and feel free to tweak the wording as you go.

I love my body and all its imperfections.

I am lovable.

I was born for this.

I have all the energy I need.

I think well on my feet.

You can write them on post-its and stick them on your mirror, fridge, or desk. Say them as often as feels right for you, out loud or in your mind, anywhere, at any time. Repeat them often for a week, check in on how you feel, and adjust as you think would be most beneficial for your personality.

Recipe for best results

All the techniques up to now will help you be your best for your personal challenge or even surpass yourself for it. For a critical challenge or event where the stakes are incredibly high for you and you're feeling the stress build, I find the following combination maximizes the impact.

☐ On the morning of the event, move in a way that reduces your baseline stress level. This could be going for a walk or run or doing any form of physical exercise. The aim is to get to a state of zen early on.

☐ Spend 5 to 10 mins or so visualizing how you will show up and act. I typically do this a few hours or a day prior to the challenge.

☐ Just before the event, play your favorite music, then do a strong REP and add any affirmation that helps boost your confidence or self-image.

☐ Then just go "rock it."

How you feel physically can also influence how you are for the event. In addition to movement, what and when you eat in advance of your challenging moment can have an influence on how you perform. This is a very individual preference and can vary depending on the challenge, especially if it's a sporting event. A word of caution is to avoid approaching a state of hypoglycemia just beforehand. Tune into your body and build self-awareness of how you perform based on your state of satiety and what and when you've eaten last.

Prepare in advance how you'll dress for the challenge and be sure to wear whatever you feel great in. It can be a jeans and t-shirt or your favorite pants and a hand-chosen top for the occasion. Wear whatever helps you feel incredible, assuming that it's somewhat appropriate for the event. This is a complete judgement call for you, as the dress code has relaxed enormously for many occasions, and people are more confident dressing in a way that's more authentic and comfortable.

Visualization doesn't necessarily take away pre-event nerves, but it will enormously increase the chances of you being or behaving as you imagined in your mind and showing up in a way that makes the difference in achieving the outcome you are aiming for. It can be even more effective when combined with the above tips. It is one of the differentiating factors between you being good on the day and you being freakin' amazing.

Your prep plan for your personal challenge

Capture the details on how you'll prepare for your personal challenge below or in your journal, and if it helps, schedule your prep in your agenda.

My personal challenge

How I'll practice

Mental preparation techniques I'll include

My empowering affirmations

What else I'll do to feel incredible on the day?

Morning visualization activity

When you get up tomorrow morning, look at your agenda and highlight what it is you are most looking to achieve during your day. I don't mean the activities, such as the meetings you are required to attend, but the outcomes you want to have achieved by the end of the day. It could be to influence your manager to assign you to a certain project, or that you close out a task you've been putting off, or doing 30 minutes of your favorite type of exercise during lunch break.

Then close your eyes, relax, and focus on your breath for a minute or two. From this relaxed state, see yourself taking the actions to achieve your outcomes, being how you need to be to get them done, and completing them well. Then tune into the associated feeling of satisfaction you get.

Do this every morning over the coming week and pay attention to the impact it has on your productivity, your self-regard, and your feeling of achievement.

End of the evening visualization activity

Part 1:

At the end of the day, sit and close your eyes. Run back over your day and your interactions in your mind. Ask yourself, "How have I been great as a parent, a partner, a friend, or colleague today?" Or ask yourself, "What did I do well today?"

See yourself in each of these moments. Feel how that fills you up. What message does this give you about you and what you want to do more of going forward? Feel the connection to the person(s) you interacted with. Feel the connection with yourself and set your intentions for the following day.

Part 2:

Run back over your day and reflect on and replay your most important interactions or events from the day in your mind. As you do so, ask yourself which of them gives you an uncomfortable feeling inside. You may have been unhappy with how you interacted with someone or how you reacted to a situation. Be compassionate with yourself and say, "At that moment and in that state, I did what I could. I'm learning from it, and I am better from this moment on." Next, in your mind, replay the same interaction with the same person(s) or replay whatever the event was and see yourself acting as you would from your higher self, this best version of you. Then, smile and tell yourself, "This is the me that is showing up as of now."

Whatever level you're currently at, Targeted Visualization can more easily get you in the zone, where your best self is your natural state of being. When you find yourself worried about anything, ask yourself if visualization can help. If yes, take a few calming minutes and see it vividly going as you want it to go, with a focus on you being how you need to be. Repetition is key, as you may be overcoming self-talk and associated ways of being that have been part of you for years. Visualize often and make it part of your preparation.

You win when nobody is watching!

CHAPTER 7

It's Not Rejection, It's Redirection

"What is this here to teach me?"
— Oprah Winfrey

"I wasn't even selected for an interview. I'm lost, and I don't know what to do."

Alizé is a bright young woman in the third year of a bachelor's degree in international business. The previous year, she came in second in her class of 160 students, so she has a good reason to be confident in her abilities. The thing is, her dream to work in fashion, either in marketing or brand management, isn't happening. A well-known fashion jewelry brand informed her that she had not been selected for an interview, and with hirings reduced due to the COVID-19 pandemic, she had fewer chances of finding work experience in the industry.

She had just declined a six-month work placement in communications, in another more technical industry, and she felt low. She said she felt lost.

I asked her, "When you say those words, 'I'm lost,' what do you feel inside?"

She answered, "Sad, anxious, and unmotivated."

"What does that do to your energy? Do you have more, less, or the same level of energy and enthusiasm to move forward?"

"Less, a lot less."

"Okay, so how about saying something different that means the same thing? Instead of 'I'm lost,' try saying, 'I'm looking for the path that's right for me.'" I gave her a moment, and she reformulated her initial expression to this new version. It was just another way of saying the same thing, of course.

"What do you feel inside this time?"

"Curious and motivated."

"And now, what does that do to your energy?"

"I feel like I have more than before. It's like I want to move forward again."

She has since found a contract in a small chain of lady's fashion boutiques to boost their online presence and is passionate about what she does. With renewed motivation she is also now pursuing acting classes to see what potential she has in that field.

In life, things don't always go the way we want them to. We don't always get what we want or what we aim for. It's just how life is. Here are some well-known examples from celebrities:

- ☐ J.K. Rowling was rejected by 12 major publishing houses for her first Harry Potter book.
- ☐ Michael Jordan wasn't selected for his high school basketball team in 10th grade and is still one of the top basketball players ever.
- ☐ Oprah Winfrey was fired from one of her first jobs, being told that she was unfit for television.

Now imagine what would have happened if Oprah decided television wasn't right for her, Michael Jordan quit basketball, or JK Rowling gave up on a possible writing career. Where would these people be now? But these people didn't let their setbacks keep them from reaching their goals.

At times, it may be that the universe is testing your will to see if that's what you really want, and you have to stand strong, maybe try a different approach, and keep going for it. It may be that the time is not yet right for a goal that size and that taking smaller steps, building your skill, and gaining life experience may be the answer for now. At times, that same universe may be giving you a message that this is not what's right for you, that this is not what you're here for. The "this" being a certain job or career, a certain person or relationship, or a goal you have. It may be that you're here for something else and you should change the course of your life.

When it doesn't work out as you wanted, from a place of peace and inner calm, take the time to reflect and ask the "Oprah question" or something similar. "What is this here to teach me?"

Why we encounter setbacks

It was a challenge, goal, or dream for which you needed to be at your best, but you didn't get the job, the guy or girl wasn't interested, you flunked the exam, you let your colleague pitch the idea instead of you, or you came in fourth in the competition. Maybe you went for your personal challenge, but it didn't work out the way you wanted.

When you look back now, what have you learned? Possibly one of the following.

- ☐ You were at your best on the day, and it just wasn't a good fit.
- ☐ Your mindset was off on the day.
- ☐ Your preparation wasn't adapted to what was needed.
- ☐ It / he / she wasn't what you truly desired, and so you had one foot on the accelerator and the other on the brake.
- ☐ You realize that this is not where you excel, at least not right now.
- ☐ There may be other reasons specific to your challenge, and with reflection you can identify what that is for you.

What was the last disappointment you experienced? When was the last time you wanted something or someone, but it didn't work out the way you hoped it would? In hindsight now, what do you think was the reason? I say in hindsight because when we are in the moment, we're often temporarily blinded to certain things when intense emotions kick in. Be it anger, fear, disappointment, or frustration, these emotions can put our rational brain in the passenger's seat and our emotional or reptilian brain is driving us. We may end up blaming our boss, our partner, or even our childhood, but that won't necessarily serve us here. Take them out of the picture and focus on who is in your sphere of control—you.

Having the ability to honestly analyze how you did or didn't prepare and how you subsequently performed will serve you for future events, assuming you do something with your insights, of course.

What can you learn from it?

So it didn't work out as you wanted it to. Here are a few questions to guide you to retrospectively look at what happened. Use whichever questions that apply to your type of situation.

- ☐ In hindsight, to what extent do you realistically see yourself as a fit for the job, client, date…and in what way would this not be the right fit for them or for you?
- ☐ What was your self-talk before and during your challenge or event?
- ☐ What, if any, mental preparation did you do in advance of the event? How did it serve you, and what would you change or add for the next similar situation?
- ☐ If you had prepared more or differently, what impact do you believe it would have had?
- ☐ How could you have shown up in a more appropriate way?
- ☐ To what extent were your intentions matched to the situation?
- ☐ What could have caused you to have your foot on the brake and not desire this as much as you may have thought?

- ☐ On a scale of 1 to 10, where does this sit as a strength for you? 10 being among the best in the company / country / world at this, 1 being your cat is probably better at this than you are.
- ☐ To what extent do you want this to happen in your career or life? If you really want it, what's your next step, and how can you accelerate your progress? (Possible options would be to get a mentor / coach, study those who excel at this, do it more often, and focus on doing one thing better each time.)

Take the answers from these questions, apply what you've learned next time, and increase your chances of getting what you aim for.

Your self-talk

Do you think JK Rowling kept telling herself, "I'm just not good enough as a writer" after the tenth publishing house rejected her book? She may have thought it, but if she kept repeating it, then chances are she never would have continued until she found one that wanted to work with her. How about you? What are you telling yourself about not getting what you aimed for?

Some of the typical things we may say to ourselves are:

- ☐ I failed the test. I'm just not smart enough.
- ☐ I lost the competition. I'm just not good enough.
- ☐ He / she left me because I'm not sexy enough.
- ☐ I knew the HR lady didn't like me. That's why they picked someone else.
- ☐ I'm really bad at speaking in public. That's why I didn't say anything. I'm so angry at myself.

When you say "I am…" followed by a negative or positive statement, and you say it often enough and with enough emotion, you start to believe it. It becomes part of who you believe you are and what your identity is. You may not get back to questioning it again, and your subconscious has you acting more in accordance with this belief of how you are. This reinforces it further, and it becomes more and more ingrained. It then influences some of your decisions in the future. When another opportunity arises, how you believe you are may determine if you decide to go for it or not.

Now, let's turn it around and say some of these energy-sucking and self-esteem bashing words in a way that still empowers us.

- ☐ I learned X, so when I retake the test, I'll be better positioned and ready.
- ☐ I didn't prepare as well as I could have. Now I better understand what works best for me to be more ready for this type of competition OR I know this sport / activity is not my number-one strength. I'm going to focus more on where I believe I have the most potential.
- ☐ He / she wasn't the right person for me. Now I'm free to find my soul mate.
- ☐ Although I didn't connect well with the HR person, I got great feedback and signals from the others. That role is best suited to someone else, as my experience on X is too light compared to what they need right now. This just means that there's another role that I'm destined for, and I'll keep working toward it.
- ☐ I'm not used to speaking in public yet, so I'll start by speaking up more in smaller groups and gradually build up to speaking in larger groups as my level of confidence grows.

Take a moment to think about the last rejection or disappointment you experienced when you didn't get what you were aiming for. What was it that you said to yourself? Was it something empowering, or did it make you feel bad about yourself? If it's the latter, flip it now.

Change your approach

If you didn't get what you aimed for, you may need to change how you approach it next time. "Sure, but what should I change?" you ask. It all starts with reflection. You're probably familiar with the expression, "Practice makes perfect." It's on the right track, for sure, as to get better at anything, you need to practice. Let's say you play golf regularly, so you are practicing your game. Will you improve? I would guess yes. Will practicing your game a few times a week help you perfect your swing as well as other elements of the game? Yes, and at the same time, I would argue that this practice alone will have you plateau in a relatively short period of time. So, what's missing?

For most challenges or skills you're looking to improve on, what's often overlooked is reflecting honestly on how you did. That may be self-reflecting or ideally also getting observations and feedback from either a coach or someone who understands the skill you're looking to build. When you get to reflect or receive feedback on how you've done, now you're going deeper. One way of doing this is to ask two questions: What did I do well? What should I work at improving or doing differently?

These are the same questions, regardless of whether you ask yourself or you're asking a person whose opinion you value.

Okay, so you understand what you did well and what to improve next time. Now what? This depends on your level of skill related to the subject at hand. The challenge can be that you don't know what you don't know. There are several options. You can find a coach, you can observe someone who excels at what you want to improve and ask them for ideas that you can apply, you can take a class, or you can check out expert online advice on YouTube. In fact, YouTube is normally my first go-to when looking to improve or learn something. And, of course, depending on the subject matter and your preferred learning style, studying a book on the subject may work for you.

Regardless of the channel you decide on, don't just look, listen, or read. The magic happens when you then apply it. Otherwise, it remains as knowledge, probably forgotten after a few weeks. To recap, reflect and either give yourself or ask for feedback, decide what you aim to continue and to improve next time, learn how to do it/ solve it, put it into practice, and then repeat the cycle.

Practice compassion with yourself

When your best friend went for something and they were disappointed for not getting it, what did you do? I'm guessing that you weren't harsh with them. You didn't knock them, criticize them, or put them down. Likely, you were compassionate with them and spoke to them with an uplifting tone. Be your own best friend here. Show the same compassion and give the same pep talk to yourself. Allow yourself space to reflect, to chill, to feel whatever negative emotions you feel. Have that glass of wine, replay that movie that you know will help lift your mood, allow yourself to feel off form for an hour or a day as you need.

Chances are that what you aimed for was outside, or on the edge of, your comfort zone. That in itself deserves congratulations. Not from me, not from friends, but from someone whose words of congratulations count most—from you to you. Yes, I do mean to congratulate yourself. Whatever it was that you aimed for, you went for it. Okay, you didn't get the result you wished for, but you went for it. Not everyone does. That alone merits giving yourself credit.

Activity: **Reflection on a Challenge**

Allow yourself a moment to connect with your thoughts and emotions, then read the questions below for your reflection and write your responses as they come to you here or in your journal.

A goal or challenge that didn't work out for me is...

One good thing that came of it is...

What I learned from it is...

What I'm congratulating myself for is...

Using that same courage, and what I've learned, what will I aim for next?

Reinforce your mindset using affirmations

After allowing yourself time to feel sad and have compassion towards yourself, let's put your mindset into a stronger place.

What affirmation or affirmations do you feel will bring out that stronger, optimistic side of you?

I've listed a few here to get you started. Pick one of these or make up your own. Just choose one you connect with, stand tall, and say it to yourself with conviction. Repeat it as often as you feel it's serving you to do so and tweak it as you go if you prefer.

- ☐ *There's something better that's destined for me.*
- ☐ *I continue to courageously expand my comfort zone.*
- ☐ *I keep advancing towards a better life.*
- ☐ *I continue to grow, learn, and improve myself every day.*
- ☐ Or, my favorite… *The best is yet to come, and I'm creating it.*

Let's recap. You would have preferred to get what you were aiming for, but it didn't go the way you wanted it to. I get it. Me too. It has happened a lot in my life and continues to happen. It's part of life, part of growing.

Be kind toward yourself, reflect, learn from it, reframe your inner words, and congratulate yourself for going outside your comfort zone. Then go for it again. Or go for something else. Just keep advancing; keep unleashing the incredible potential you possess. You are unique, and so is the amazing impact that you can make. Your time here is short. Keep making it count. Remember, what you experienced wasn't rejection; it was simply redirection.

Imposter syndrome

Before ending Part 1 of the book, there's one more subject to consider. It's not about not getting what you want, or aimed for; rather, the opposite. You improved yourself, prepared for it, and achieved it. You got the role, the guy or girl, the title, or the recognition, and now you feel like you're not deserving of it. You feel like you just got lucky and that sooner or later, you'll be found out. Lots of us don't feel like we merit what we have achieved and how far we have come.

Imposter syndrome is loosely defined as feeling like a fraud and not being good enough, and it's something most people are familiar with.

Those with imposter syndrome have difficulty internalizing their success and accepting praise as valid. They often attribute their success to external factors, such as having gotten lucky or their competitors not performing well on that day. They not only discount positive feedback and objective evidence of success but also develop arguments to prove that they do not deserve praise or credit for particular achievements.

A primary difference between those who feel like imposters and those who don't is not their intelligence or capabilities but what they think about themselves and what they focus on.

Some of the techniques we've discussed so far will help you overcome imposter syndrome if this is something you're experiencing.

Targeted Visualization
See yourself repeatedly performing at your best.

Your Wow List
Recognize your strengths and qualities and review your list often.

Compliments Journal

To compliment your Wow List, keep adding to and regularly reviewing your journal.

Your Victory List of Successes
Stop minimizing what you achieve, write down your successes, and allow yourself moments of celebration. Note, not all of your successes come down to luck!

Affirmations
Use strong affirmations to reinforce your self-image (repetition is one of the ways our subconscious learns).

Reframing
Ask a question such as, "What are the qualities they see in me, for them to choose me?"

Regularly practicing these techniques will help flip your focus to a more positive and competent version of who you are and help you to stop doubting your abilities. See yourself in a more positive light, understand why you deserve what you achieved, and enhance your sense of self-worth.

PART 2

STRONG THROUGH CHALLENGING TIMES

CHAPTER 8

———

An Instant Remedy

"Reality is created by the mind.
We can change our reality
by changing our mind."
— Plato

The phone rang. It was my little sister. "Did you hear the news?"

"No, what?"

"Dad just left!"

"What do you mean?"

"He left Mom! He's gone!"

WTF!

After my parents had been married for 49 years, our family unit shattered at that moment.

The bottom had fallen out from under my world.

My father felt that they weren't getting on anymore, and he couldn't handle it.

As I am the eldest in a family of four siblings, I found that keeping the peace between everyone and trying to keep the family together as much as possible was resting on my shoulders. And it wasn't an easy task. I was consciously looking to see things from both sides. I'd spent 15 years living abroad and was used to seeing high levels of divorce and separation among those of my parents' generation. Despite this rational view, emotionally, I felt torn.

Have you ever had a deep-felt desire to cry, just surging up from inside after getting news of something, but resisted and held it in? This was one of those times.

That is, until I had my mom on the phone a little while later. Her tears of despair just opened my floodgates, especially after our telephone conversation ended.

It had been a long time since I shed so many tears and asked myself so many heart-wrenching questions. "How could he do this?" "Why didn't they get couples therapy?" "How will Mom cope with living alone?"

On the phone to my family, I had to be strong and diplomatic. As I said, I'm the eldest sibling of the clan.

"How can I stay strong and positive with all this going on?" I asked myself.

A couple of months later, my phone rang again.

It was my sister this time.

"A notorious convicted drug dealer has just moved into the apartment attached to the house where Mom is living, and he has a violent history," at least according to media reports she found on the Internet.

Silence on both sides of the line.

Another *WTF!! Is this really happening?*

A couple years earlier, my mom was diagnosed with lymphoma, which is cancer of the lymph nodes. She had just been given a green light after receiving chemotherapy, followed by her first radiation therapy, and for now had the all-clear from her oncologist, at least for the months to come.

How will she get through this separation? Will she even survive it? She was distraught with sadness and hurt. Another incredible and unwanted stressful event had been put in her life.

Feeling weighed down by all of this bad news had me looking for a way to stay mentally and emotionally strong and resilient. I felt the pressure of needing to be available for my family and also stay focused on my job, while trying to accept what had happened.

Intense moments thinking, *I really can't take any more bad news* and *What the hell is going to come next?*

I didn't want to talk to anyone who tended to focus on negative elements of what was happening in their life. I was feeling too weighed down by what was now happening in mine.

I couldn't take any more of life's downsides to the point that, at times, I let my phone ring out without answering. The chances were high that the person on the other end would just drop a negativity bomb, and I felt I couldn't handle any more bad news.

Ever been there?

It was around then that I started to really experiment with visualization, gratitude, and meditation, seeking the "miracle solution" that would help me shoulder all these challenging events and not crumble.

Boosting my level of resilience and optimism was primordial. I needed to cross over that line, from feeling down to where life's not bad, to where life freakin' rocks again. I needed it for me, for those I loved, and even needed it to stay effective in my job.

Target in sight. Now how to get there?

At this moment in time, what was most beneficial to feel lighter and more positive again was focusing on gratitude.

Why gratitude?

Research shows that grateful people tend to be happier people. Practicing gratitude lowers levels of stress and helps you cope better with adversity. It enhances empathy and reduces aggression. It helps foster resilience, reduces social comparisons, and improves self-esteem. It can even help you sleep better.

When you're not in a good place, it's challenging to get back to a neutral level, never mind trying to achieve something great in your work or your life. For me, this was the logic in starting with gratitude first. I had to create and build on a solid, more positive state of mind, then go on and work from there to achieve whatever was important for me.

The results felt incredibly good and reassuring. I became happier and more satisfied with life in an amazingly short period of time.

Sometimes when I would go into a gratitude exercise, I felt weighed down by life's occasional bullsh*t periods, but when I came out the other side, despite all the stuff that could feel overwhelming at times, I knew that I was living a beautiful life!

I could feel a warm sensation coming from inside, which I had never experienced in the past. A reassuring, heart-warming sensation. It was like starting off from a state of being worn down, closed, and somewhat bitter about how life is at the moment to ending the session feeling lighter, with a gentle forward-moving energy, almost pulling me towards creating more moments to feel grateful for. My mind was filled with so many good images that somehow the problems in my mind started to shrink. The problems were still there, of course, but it was like there was a buffer of beautiful moments and caring people between me and those problems, like a cushion to soften the blow. This is what I focused on—precious moments and the loving people in my life. It was like starting off feeling empty and almost hopeless to feeling filled back up to a certain extent and seeing the balance that exists in life between challenge and joy once more.

Even after the first gratitude session, I was able to go back and have difficult and constructive conversations with family members about what happened. I was back answering the phone again to those people who also needed to talk about their challenges, at least in small doses.

It helped me to converse with them and focus on finding solutions, rather than getting bogged down by everything negative that could have been said about the recent events.

The wheel had started to turn in the direction of better times once more.

How to practice gratitude

You can practice gratitude anywhere and at any time, eyes open or eyes closed, in your mind or in a journal.

I've done this on the train, lying in bed, walking in nature, taking a shower, waiting in a cafe for a friend…the list is endless. My favorite time and place is on my mat after exercising. This really puts me in a good place.

Simply think of nice moments, events, or people in your life that you could express appreciation for, and say thank you for them.

To add depth, step into each moment or see each person in your mind's eye. See the moment or person, feel the gratitude in your heart, say thank you to the universe, and then move onto the next one. It's beyond just saying what you're grateful for in words.

Instead of just saying thanks for the hug from your child or partner this morning before leaving for work, play that film in your mind, go back and relive that beautiful moment, feel what you felt then, and then add a "thank you."

Same thing if you capture this in a journal. See the moment or the person in your mind before or as you write what you're grateful for. I do use a journal at times, though most often, I practice gratitude in my mind without capturing it in writing.

Writing what you're grateful for in a journal does have additional benefits, though. For instance, my youngest daughter, Malorie, would stay with me occasionally on Friday evenings. Before we'd go to sleep, I'd pull out a leather-covered notebook and ask if she wanted to capture what she felt grateful for.

On most occasions, she'd agree, so I'd hand her the notebook and pen and let her go first.

When she was done, she'd hand it back, and I'd flip it around and write on the back pages. Then, and this was a magic moment for me, we'd read each other's text.

Such a beautiful moment of sharing.

There is an additional benefit of writing it down, which I discovered just recently. I was spring cleaning the house and picked up the notebook. It felt like what I'd call a "double dopamine hit." By rereading what we had captured months earlier, I was able to relive some of those moments and feel an incredible sensation of gratitude again.

Neuroscientific research on gratitude shows that when we express gratitude and receive the same, our brain releases dopamine and serotonin, the two crucial neurotransmitters responsible for our emotions, and they make us feel "good." They enhance our mood immediately, making us feel happy from the inside.

A good friend of mine recently started having gratitude conversations at the dinner table with his family. He started asking each family member what they felt grateful for from their day. Now, to his surprise and delight, occasionally his teenagers initiate the conversation. His words to me were, "It's such a great bonding moment with each other and an incredible habit to have as a family."

What do you feel grateful for?

What do you or could you feel grateful for? Someone you love in your life, maybe a partner, a parent, a child, or a friend? Or how about a special moment that brought you or a loved one joy, even just for a passing instant? A kiss from your partner when you arrive home? A compliment that you received from a colleague? A job you appreciate, or being physically able to do what you can do? Your child being happy about their school test results?

If you can't find something to be grateful for, then start by changing your energy to one where you can more easily feel grateful in your heart for what or who's in your life. Listen to inspiring or relaxing music that will uplift you or calm you. Move, walk, run, or do whatever it is that gets you to connect with your heart. Go somewhere that is special or has meaning for you. Take a wander on a beach or a walk in nature. Sit in silence in a church, synagogue, or mosque. Visit someone who's alone in a hospital. Ask others what they feel grateful for and get inspired by their stories.

Look outside of yourself and see what you can be grateful for with regard to the circumstances of those that you love, your family, your friends, colleagues. It doesn't always have to be about you. Feel the gratitude for them, and even, without wanting to sound esoteric, send them good energy.

It's not normally part of my practice, but on occasion, I've imagined sending calming or healing energy to someone I care for and it having an effect on their health. During a recent practice, I was feeling gratitude for my favorite uncle, an incredible human being, who wasn't well. I sat in a rather meditative state and imagined healing energy going from my hands to him and being absorbed by his body. It can be an emotional experience and rather intense and is something I add to my practice only when I feel a certain pull, state of mind, and energy.

When it doesn't feel easy...

If you still cannot think of anything, then allow me to give you a little wake up call. If you have the privilege of being where you are, and are reading this book, there's a high probability that someone, somewhere, on another part of the planet, even in another part of your city, would dream of the life you have.

Now if you position yourself as that person, ask yourself, "What would they be envious of when they see my life that I'm possibly taking for granted?" It's a possible starting point for you to focus on.

I recently felt I needed some inspiration and had a hard time feeling grateful. I ended up sitting in silence in God's house to see what that brought up in me. I went to church, to the Strasbourg Cathedral to be precise.

Though it had been a while since I'd been in such a religious place, I could still sense the familiarity of it and paid my respects upon entering.

From previous visits as a tourist, I was aware that they cordoned off an area for pilgrims to sit in private prayer or reflection. This is where I sat in silence. I could feel the peaceful surroundings and iconic holy figures quieting my racing mind.

I felt so grateful that my eyes were tearing up with intense emotion, feeling blessed for the life I have and for those whom I am privileged to share this journey with.

These minutes spent focusing on heart-warming images had me leaving there feeling calm, appreciative, and inspired to find, and create, more to be grateful for in my life, and in the lives of those I love.

Gratitude Activity

Sit in silence for a moment, your eyes open or closed, and ask yourself, "For what or whom do I feel grateful for today?"

To bring it to another level, when you think of a person, zoom in on what you appreciate about them and let this be the focus of your gratitude for them. Say thank you for the impact they have on you and on others.

When you think back to a special moment, step into it again in your mind and relive it. Allow your facial gestures to express what you feel as you do so.

Feel the calming of the mind and lightening of the spirit that this activity brings you.

Afterwards, in the space below, if you wish, write out what and for whom you feel grateful for today...

Take a minute to introspect and reflect on the following questions.

How does that gratitude exercise make you feel inside?

How does that make you feel about your life or life in general?

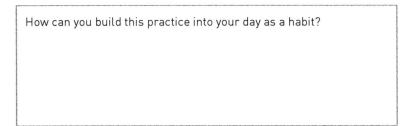

How can you build this practice into your day as a habit?

My habit has been to incorporate it into the end of my workouts, where I sit on my mat and go through a guided meditation that starts with gratitude practice.

Because this was happening only three to four times a week, and I wanted to focus on what I was grateful for every day, I've since created a new habit around it. Now, when my feet touch the ground in the morning as I get out of bed, I sit or I kneel down and I rest my elbows on the mattress and say thank you for everything I feel grateful for in my life or that occurred in the life of someone I love.

If I miss this practice for some reason, my deal with myself is that I cannot look at anything on social media until I do my gratitude practice. This catches me up in case I got out of bed and forgot to do my habit, due to my thoughts being elsewhere.

A last word. When you start appreciating what you have in your life today, the people, the moments, the lifestyle, you may find that you'll tend to experience less frustration, less envy, and less regret. It can make you feel more optimistic and fulfilled, and you'll see your overall mood improve.

Practicing gratitude also helps us to come out of self-pity. It changes our mindset from "poor me," to one that says, "You know what? Despite all of the BS going on in my life at the moment, I still have a beautiful life. Thank you!"

To close out this chapter, I would like to return to my family story.

My parents are both beautiful people, but like lots of us, they just didn't do the right things for their marriage to work. Mom could live with it; Dad couldn't.

They've since adapted their lifestyles and continue to live separate lives, while spending time with their children and grandchildren. I will always love them both.

The former drug dealer turned out to be a nice guy. My mom appreciated him, and he hugged her when he moved on a year later.

As for Mom's health, she was determined to beat the cancer and win her life back. That was more than five years ago. She went for another radiation treatment as prescribed. She changed her eating habits to include making raw juices every day, cutting way down on meat, and eating less sugar. She started walking more and has to date beaten off the return of the dreaded C word.

I feel so grateful every day for my mom's inner strength. So grateful for her still being here. She surprised herself more than anyone else. She never saw herself as strong, but as the saying goes, "You don't know how strong you are until being strong is your only option." Well done, Mom! You did it! You're still here today to give your gentle, incredible love to your family, and say a kind word to those you encounter.

My dad has carried on with his life on another path and continues to work today at almost 75. He's worked since he was 14 years old and will do as long as he's able. An ex-rugby player with a big heart, he's taught me to go and do it and not make any excuses.

As for me, I am committed to practicing gratitude as a lifelong, daily habit, like brushing my teeth. I am forever amazed at the benefits gained from simply focusing on those moments that I appreciate and cherish, as well as on the beautiful people I am blessed to have in my life. It costs nothing, takes very little time, and it can be done anytime, anywhere. Life is full of surprises, some nice and others challenging, at least initially. Discovering gratitude and its benefits has definitely been a nice surprise. A welcome surprise. Thank you, life.

To you, the reader, I wish you so much to be grateful for in your life and that you get to feel it in your heart. It's such an incredible way to start or end each day.

Gratitude is such a powerful technique that we'll refer to it in several contexts in the pages that follow.

Next, let's look at what you can do about the challenging and often unpredictable surprises that life brings.

CHAPTER 9

Change Your Story

"I don't like to lose at anything.
Yet I've grown most not from victories,
but setbacks."
— Serena Williams

You return home one day to learn that your partner has decided to leave you. Despite the fact that you really haven't been getting along well over the last few months, you're taken aback and feel sad, angry, and empty on the inside.

As a result, you lack the desire to socialize and you spend significantly more time at home than you normally do, feeling sorry for yourself. While on the phone with a friend, you blame and belittle your partner. You begin to doubt your suitability as a life partner, and your confidence suffers.

As a consequence, you end up having a few casual relationships with people who are clearly not your type but do so out of a combination of low self-esteem and boredom. This makes you feel even worse about yourself and your life, and you stop dating entirely, reverting to a form of needy pleading with your ex-partner to reconcile. They do feel sorry for you, but only to a point. They won't take you back.

In the above example, we've established that an event occurs…

It causes you to feel a certain way.

What you feel then determines what you do and if or when you do it.

This action then gives you a certain result, possibly one you desire, or possibly one that you would have preferred to avoid.

This flow reads as…

Event → Feeling → Action → Result

Reread the above flow and see whether you agree with it. Are you aware of this pattern in your own life? If you answered yes, then you are…wrong! And this is one of the times where you being wrong is excellent news. In fact, it's awesome news.

Allow me to explain. This is a critical point.

Between the event and how you feel is the story you tell yourself about the event. It's not the event that determines how you feel. Your interpretation or story of the event is what elicits certain emotions in you. It's that story you tell yourself about what happened that matters.

That's great news, as you are the one that gets to control your story. That's the freakin' awesome news, in fact. That's what puts us in the driver seat so we are not at the mercy of life's unpredictable and random events. We can't always control life events or when they occur, but we do control our interpretation of those events; we do control the story we tell ourselves about each event.

This true flow reads as…

Event → Interpretation → Feeling → Action → Result

Why was the person whose partner abandoned them feeling sad, angry, and so on? It's because of the story they told themselves about being broken up with by their partner. This is, at least in part, what created these emotions. It could go something like this:

- ☐ "I've never lived alone and despite our frequent disagreements, I wish they would stay. I can't handle being alone."
- ☐ "I'll never find anyone as good / interesting / cute / nice ... as them again."
- ☐ "Without them, my life is incomplete."
- ☐ "It'll appear to others that I wasn't good enough for them."

Now let's look at what changing to a more empowering story would look like for the situation above.

You come home one day, and your partner announces they are leaving you. Both of you are aware that you really haven't been getting along well over this last while.

Your story or interpretation this time is: "We haven't been well together these last few months. We've been arguing all the time despite several attempts to improve things. It's extremely stressful to be in this situation, and it's been affecting my mood and my work. I guess we're not as compatible as I thought. I'm glad he / she had the courage to make that decision. I'm sure there's someone out there whom I'm more compatible with."

The result is that you value the newly found "you time" without the stress from the relationship you had and devote it to a new activity you've been meaning to begin. At the same time, you appreciate your friends being there and invest in creating stronger bonds with them. You also spend time analyzing what went wrong in your relationship and how to be a better partner for the next person in your life.

The outcome is that you feel more grounded and wiser, and you won't be in a hurry to meet anyone just yet, which can be an attractive trait.

One day, unexpectedly, you are introduced to someone. You feel a spark, and they are attracted to the new improved version of you... You understand the upside of your partner leaving and are thankful that they did.

I agree that it's slightly exaggerated and has a fairytale feel to it, but do you notice the difference?

Same event; different story or interpretation. Change your story, and your life will change.

Let's look at an example that isn't a fairytale…

When the COVID-19 lockdown was announced, a lot of people went into a state of mild panic. Outside, lines formed for food and other necessities at collection points. I recall seeing a man with two shopping carts full of nothing but water bottles and toilet paper. Incredible! Then I heard about a local pizzeria owner who was delivering free pizza to local hospitals' front-line medical staff. What a distinction. Lockdown was the same event for both of these gentlemen, but their reactions were completely different. Whatever the toilet paper hoarder was thinking to himself or asking himself, it was certainly not the same as the pizzeria owner's thoughts. I'm guessing the latter asked himself something along the lines of, "How can I use this for the greater good?" And he acted on his answer.

"That's fine," I hear you say, "but it's a common reaction to start telling ourselves all the things that could go wrong." You'd be correct. Our brain, after all, is designed to keep us safe above all else. This entails avoiding risk, and one way it accomplishes this is by focusing our attention on the negative, on what could go wrong. That way, we'll be able to avoid the risk and stay safe. According to my observations, we usually begin with a disempowering story, due to the negativity bias in our brains, and then consciously need to turn it around in our favor.

By asking ourselves better questions, we can overcome this and help our brains see the great options and possibilities that still exist, despite the current challenge. Yes, you may first need time and space before being able to stand back from what just happened and reframe it. Take the space and then ask one or more of the questions below.

- ☐ "What good can I find in this?"
- ☐ "If it happened to my best friend, what would I advise them to focus on or to do here?" Then follow your own advice.
- ☐ "What else could this mean?"
- ☐ "How can I put this to use for the greater good?"
- ☐ "What can I learn from it?"

Let's take a look at some of these in action, beginning with identifying any positive outcomes from the situation.

What good can you find in this?

I just parked my car in our company parking lot, and my phone rang. It was the father of my friend Jacinta. It was a short conversation, and all I recall from it is: "Jacinta is not in a good place. I fear that she's going into a depression."

You see, Jacinta, at that point, hadn't eaten any solid food in about two years. I remember calling her one day and asking how she was. "Not great" was the answer.

"Why? What's going on with you?"

"When I eat, the food comes back up."

"You mean acid reflux, right? Stomach acid coming up."

"No, I mean the food!"

I was at a loss for words.

In essence, the muscle at the end of her esophagus would no longer open sufficiently to let the food down. After lots of extremely uncomfortable tests and several medical interventions, nothing had worked to reverse the situation, and after one intervention, she came out of hospital with an additional condition, one that she didn't have prior to the intervention. It was later diagnosed as a form of trigeminal neuralgia, a severe facial pain in the jaw, teeth, or gums.

The day after her father informed me of his concern for her, she called. She was distraught. She was having a really hard time physically and emotionally and now was literally crying out for help. I could feel myself starting to tear up and so I stepped outside of my office building. I was racking my brain. *How can I help?* She was in despair.

Outside the office building on this cloudy morning, colleagues were walking by, going about their working day, and I felt the intensity of our conversation. My friend explained all that was going on and sounded like there was no hope for the quality of her life to improve.

Then I asked what appeared to be the most stupid, naive question possible. "What good has come of this unimaginably painful situation?"

"What? What kind of question is that? I've lost almost 20 kilos and still cannot eat any solid food. I drool at the mouth when I see others eating. I have bouts of incredible face pain, at times cannot even brush my teeth or drive, and I'll never be able to work again. And you're asking what's positive about it!"

I felt terrible, and at the same time, I knew that I had to persist. We had to swing around this negative spiral going on in her mind.

"Yes, I know it sounds crazy. The thing is that you tried everything to change the physical conditions with several doctors, and they only made it worse. If you can't change the event, the only thing I see possible is to change how you see the event."

"I don't see anything that's positive about it."

Holding back my tears, I said, "You get to spend more time with your sons, right?"

"Yes, but I'm not often in a good mood due to the pain."

"Yes, but you didn't get to see them much with your long working hours previously."

"True."

"What else?"

"I don't know."

Grasping at straws, I cringed and suggested, "You did want to lose weight for years, right?"

"Yeah, but I lost 20 kilos and now I'm really skinny." She normally has an incredible sense of humor, and now I could hear a glimmer of a sarcastic laugh appearing in her voice.

Then I asked again, "What else? Even something small."

"Well, I can fit into clothes now that I never could before."

"Great, now keep asking yourself that same question, and other answers will come to you. Plus, please write down the positives we just mentioned. Like that, you'll have that list at your fingertips when you feel you need it most."

Jacinta and others with serious health conditions are true heroes, and we will never truly know what they go through. Being able to reframe can help some of our heroes find relief and uplift their mental and emotional states.

This is a real-life example of this question in action. It sounds simple, but it works!

If you can't change your circumstances or an event that just occurred, you can change your perspective on it. Yes, in many cases, the benefit is insignificant in comparison to the pain. The question is, what happens if you continuously focus on the pain and what you've lost? It's a recipe for depression. Find something positive to focus on as a result of the event, however small or trivial it may appear at first. Remember, what we focus on expands.

What would you ask or advise your best friend?

Let's say you just had an oral exam in front of a panel of judges for a class you've been taking. You got off to a good start but were caught off guard by one panel member, who is known for asking extremely difficult questions that destabilize even the most well-prepared. Not just with his words, but also with an almost aggressive tone, and all of this in front of his peers. You lose your composure and give a half-hearted response that doesn't really satisfy him. You move on quickly. You finish strong, and the majority of the panel appear to be impressed by your mastery of the subject in question.

On your drive home after the exam, you reflect on what happened.

"I'm such an idiot. How could I allow myself to be so thrown off? He made me look completely unprepared in front of everyone. Why did I react so stupidly?"

Now, imagine it was your best friend who made that same presentation. What would your discussion look like? Something for you to think about: How long would you remain friends if you said the same things to them as you just said to yourself? Not very long, I would bet.

To emphasize the point, here's what that would sound like, if you spoke to them in the same way you spoke to yourself.

"You're such an idiot. How could you let yourself be thrown off like that? He made you look really foolish in front of everyone. Why did you react so stupidly?"

Now to be fair, it's not always easy to step back and speak to yourself like you were speaking to your best friend in that same situation, particularly if you're in a highly charged emotional state. What I suggest is to go for a walk, or do an activity to get you to de-stress first, and from that more relaxed state, flip it. Then ask how you would speak to your friend, or what questions would you ask them, if it happened to them. Then speak to yourself in the same manner.

"What else could this mean?"

Another question that can help you take back control and find a new interpretation to get you into a better emotional place is "What else could this mean?"

To give you another example: Have you ever lost your job? Maybe you weren't a good fit for your newly assigned role? Or you didn't get along with your manager or new boss? Or you've been part of a downsizing? It's not a great feeling, right? Again, how we feel depends on our interpretation and on the story we tell ourselves upon hearing the news.

- ☐ "It must be that I'm not good enough."
- ☐ "I should have done more of x or less of y."
- ☐ "I knew I wasn't good enough for the role. They eventually discovered the truth." (classic imposter syndrome)

I was recently impacted by both a company reorganization and also by being the wrong fit for an extremely dictatorial manager. Did I start by telling myself these confidence-sucking stories? You bet I did, and I felt all the worse for it.

The last time it happened to me, after the initial shock had passed, I asked myself the question: "What else could this mean?"

I should warn you that the answer doesn't always come immediately. Simply repeat the question several times to yourself, and a part of your brain will continue searching. It may appear at a completely unpredictable moment. From nowhere, the answer you're seeking may pop up while you are driving your car, in the middle of a run, or taking a shower.

The answer I found about losing my job was, "I've been in this role for too long and now I really need to get out of my comfort zone and grow."

Boom! What an insight! Simple, yet effective. I needed to move my butt, learn new skills, and surround myself with new people. If I didn't, in any case, I'd almost certainly lose my job later, as I'd surely become obsolete.

Create a virtuous cycle

When you feel powerless and tell yourself a negative story about your situation, your energy and enthusiasm can plummet, and a vicious cycle can begin. You begin to feel more helpless in the face of this tragic situation in your life, and your energy levels take a nosedive. Being in this low-energy state feels like it's reducing your ability to see things clearly and reclaim an empowered mindset. This depletes your energy even more, and so the spiral continues. This can be aggravated further by telling almost everyone you meet about your sorry state of affairs, or at least your version of it.

The above questions will help you swing this around and replace it with a virtuous cycle that is uplifting. Begin this virtuous cycle by doing something that will change your state. A walk, a brief meditation, or any form of movement or exercise will help you get into a more powerful state of mind from which to think and from which to ask one of the powerful reframing questions and see things from a more helpful angle. The answer to the question can help you take back control, which, in turn, will give you increased energy, and the cycle is now uplifting.

Some of the examples above are not common occurrences for most of us, so before you practice, let's make a list of a few more commonly occurring events we might encounter.

- ☐ A colleague received the promotion you were expecting
- ☐ You didn't make the grade
- ☐ You lost the match
- ☐ Your son / daughter failed their math exam
- ☐ You didn't get the bonus you were counting on

YES YOU *Frenkin'* CAN

☐ You didn't get selected for the team
☐ You just lost a customer…

Now it's your turn...

Activity: Reframing a Tough Event

Let's do an activity to put this into action.

List an event that you believe is currently causing you to feel a negative emotion, write in the table below or in your journal, the story you've been telling yourself about it, and then answer the questions that follow. If you don't have such an event in life currently, select a recent one.

The tough event

What is the story I've been telling myself about it?

How is that making me feel?

What would I advise my best friend to focus on or to do here?

What good can I find in this?

What else could this mean?

How can I use this?

How is this new, more empowering story, formulated from answering the above questions, making me feel?

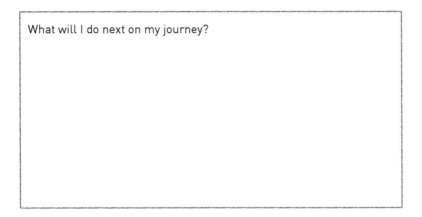

What will I do next on my journey?

We don't have control over the majority of life's events, but we do have control over how we interpret them. Even if the initial interpretation is overwhelmingly negative, we can change it by asking empowering questions.

Better questions lead to better answers. Better answers lead to better feelings. Better feelings lead to a better life.

CHAPTER 10

Keep Your Glass Topped Up

"Talk to yourself like you'd talk to someone you love."
— Bréné Brown

Have you ever seen a glass of wine stay full for long?

Let us pretend for a moment that the wine represents your resilience, and you represent the glass. When it starts to run low, you, your host, or the person you're with will take the bottle and top it up, right?

In our analogy, what does the bottle represent? It's a symbol for all those things we can do to boost our inner strength.

Do I mean that you should drink wine in order to be resilient? No, of course not, though there's nothing wrong with an occasional glass of wine. Stay with me now. In this chapter, we'll look at how to build and maintain a base level of resilience that will help you get through life's little challenges. This also acts as a starting point for bringing your resilience to a peak level for life's bigger challenges, as we'll cover in the next chapter.

What are the benefits of you keeping your proverbial glass topped up?

Having a high base level of resilience is what gives us that advantageous starting point from which we can handle what life can, at times, throw at us.

It helps us get over the smaller stressful events that accumulate. You know, the stuff that we've forgotten about a week later, but when they occur, they draw on our inner reserves.

It also helps boost our confidence in ourselves and in our future, strengthening our belief that whatever happens, we will manage and be stronger or wiser because of it. A word here on the wiser element. In order for this to happen, we need to invest time in self-reflection. More on this in Chapter 12.

Being wiser also means knowing when your glass is being emptied and when you should put a conscious focus on topping it up again.

What else can resilience do for us? It can help us step up and ask for that promotion, or go for something we want, knowing that if we don't get it, we're going to be OK. Our armor hasn't been dented.

With a certain level of resilience, we can ask questions like, "If I can be courageous and go for it, and not be badly impacted if it doesn't work out, what else can I do or try? What else will I do or try?"

When something doesn't go the way you want it to, it won't drain your glass, as it was pretty full to begin with.

So, let's keep that glass filled to a level such that when tough life events start to drain it, you have enough to keep you above that positive life-energy line.

Be careful what you fill it with

Before we go on, you probably know that there's good quality fine wine and pretty much something that resembles vinegar.

In a similar way, concerning your mindset, some activities are like having a glass of a high-quality Chardonnay, which you appreciate and savor. Others have the unwanted effects of lower-quality wines, those that will give you a bad hangover the next day from even having a glass or two.

Such lower quality activities to avoid include things like…

- ☐ Accepting advice from someone who doesn't have your best interest at heart
- ☐ Beating yourself up with what you say to yourself. This can sound like: "Why is my life so difficult?"
- ☐ Trying to change something that's entirely out of your control
- ☐ Hanging out with people who are jealous of you or what your life is like
- ☐ Overindulging in stuff you know is bad for you in the long run

We're going to focus only on high-end or high-quality resilience boosters. Let's start with who you hang out with.

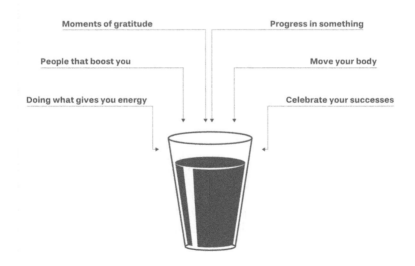

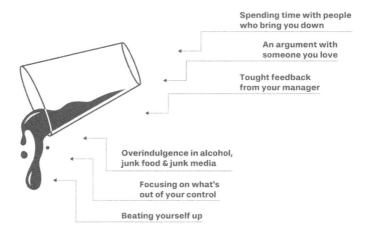

Spending time with people
who bring you down

An argument with
someone you love

Tought feedback
from your manager

Overindulgence in alcohol,
junk food & junk media

Focusing on what's
out of your control

Beating yourself up

Who are your top 5?

There is an expression that says you become the average of the five people you spend most time with. I'm not sure where the number five came from, but I do believe in the idea.

Think about it for a moment. If you spend a lot of time with people that swear a lot, then chances are that your vocabulary expands to include more expletives than before. If your best friend talks a lot about current affairs, then you start to follow the news more, even just to be able to have a two-way conversation with them.

So how does this relate to my resilience levels? If you hang out with negative and pessimistic people a lot, then guess what? You become more negative and pessimistic also. This phenomenon is known in psychology as emotional contagion. According to the *Harvard Business Review,* "It starts when we automatically mimic other people's facial expressions, body language, tone of voice—which we're hardwired to do from infancy. What happens next is also 'infectious': Through a variety of physiological and neurological processes, we actually feel the emotions we mimicked—and then act on them." This can be the case with both negative and positive emotions.

Let me give you a couple of examples.

I have a colleague who has an incredibly positive, uplifting energy, and when we are around each other, her positive energy rubs off on me. I end up being more positive and optimistic in what I think and say, and I smile more, thanks to her.

On the other hand, I used to work with a colleague who was very cynical and negative. When we'd speak with each other, it sucked away most of my positivity, and I'd feel drained afterward. He would find something negative to say about practically everything. We would often have lunch together, and I found myself becoming influenced by him and being more negative and critical during our lunch conversations. Just as bad is that it also carried into my own time when lunch was over, and it started to become a habit.

What happens to your energy when you are pessimistic about something? It drops, right?

Let's try this right now and get pessimistic for a moment. I promise to bring you back to an optimistic place right after. Think of a challenging situation for you. Find or create a story around what's negative about it and harp on about it. Say your pessimistic thoughts out loud, as if you were venting to a friend.

Take note of where your energy is at when you are pessimistic and complaining like that. It's tough to be resilient when your energy is in that place.

Now, let's do the opposite. Think of the same challenging situation but adopt an optimistic perspective. Say all of the things you can do to get to a better place. Talk about everything that's positive that you can find in this situation.

Again, take note of where your energy is at when you are positive and optimistic like that.

Do you feel the difference? Who in your life is influencing you to be more positive or at least more objective? And who is influencing you in the opposite direction? I am not saying to stop spending time with negative or pessimistic people, but at least try to spend more time with those who are more positive and optimistic, especially at key moments for you. Your level of optimism and your level of resilience are related. Spend more time with optimistic people and see how your outlook and energy change.

Remember that this works both ways, so it helps to be aware of the type of energy you are giving to others. The more you complain and criticize, the more you tilt that glass yourself and your resilience level starts to drain. Resist the temptation to complain to others and to look for validation from them that you have a reason to complain. This will only reinforce a negative downward spiral for you.

To become more optimistic, use the techniques in this book, such as creating your Victory List of successes, visualizing the outcome you want, reframing negative self-talk, practicing gratitude, and using positive affirmations.

This doesn't mean that you need to be optimistic at every moment of every day. We are human, after all. While it's good for our mental health and resilience to see the positive in situations, if you refuse to acknowledge the negative, you put yourself at risk for being in denial about your current reality, so it's all about balance. I believe in understanding the reality of a challenge, taking the time to acknowledge and accept your related emotions, and then focusing on what you can do to move forward.

By the way, there's an added bonus to being optimistic. As well as boosting your inner strength reserves, being optimistic can also help you live longer. Scientists from Harvard and Boston Universities recently published results from data on 70,000 people and concluded that just by being an optimist you can extend your life by 14.9 percent on average.

Acknowledge and celebrate your successes

Let's say you helped your child with their homework, while remaining calm and explaining things well, despite the constant impatient twitching and the "I don't care about this stupid homework" expressions coming at you from the little person you're helping, and you kept the commitment you made to yourself to go on a run after work, even though you didn't sleep well the night before, and you really felt like just sitting in front of the TV with your favorite snack food... For most of us, we continue our day or evening without a second thought to what we've just done. If it was your partner or friend that did that, chances are that you'd recognize it with words. And these are perceived as small, almost unnoticed wins. What I'm suggesting here is to recognize the successes you have, however big or small, and allow yourself moments of celebration.

Here are some ideas as to how you could celebrate.

☐ Share a moment of appreciation with someone that helped make it possible.

☐ As soon as you've done it, whatever it is, give yourself a dopamine hit. For example, smile or say a high-energy "Yes," while making a powerful gesture. This is a great anchor moment, so create that anchor by squeezing your thumb and a fingertip together. You can use this again later to recreate that positive, confident feeling when you need it.

☐ Do something spontaneous and unplanned, alone or with a loved one.

☐ Treat yourself to a massage, dinner in your favorite restaurant, a glass of your favorite beverage...or all of the above. :-) During this pleasurable experience, be sure to focus on what you did well.

☐ At the very least, reflect on what you did well, maybe just before you fall off to sleep that evening. Then smile and gently fall into sleep.

Activity: Evening Reflection

At the end of the day, ask yourself and answer questions like…

☐ "What did I handle well today?"
☐ "What can I congratulate myself for today?"
☐ "What have I learned about myself?"

Then give yourself an uplifting complement and smile.

Pre-determine your media focus

Though we cannot control most of what happens around us, if we don't take control of which media content we choose to focus on, we can add more daily stress in our lives, and more daily stress means emptying that glass drop by drop.

News coverage, for the most part, highlights what's ugly, unjust, and shocking in our world. I'm not judging the media here, as they need to get our attention; I'm just bringing our awareness to the choices we make and the effects of watching and listening to certain news coverage and social media feeds. Watching up-close coverage of horrific events will not help us maintain a strong mental state. I'm not saying to ignore important news updates, but do we need to watch this day in, day out? If you need to stay up to date, maybe just watching or reading the headlines will do it for you. Or decide to watch the news on replay so you get to choose what you fast forward and what you spend time on.

Take note of what media coverage or social media channels amplify your stress and anxieties and ignore, delete, or minimize these outlets. You have the power to choose what you let into your conscious mind. Regardless of what happens in the outside world, you and only you get to choose what you allow into your inner world.

How active is your news filter right now? Is it time to readjust the settings? Thinking about what it is you want before you select a channel, program, social media feed, or YouTube video and connecting your finger to your emotional desire will ensure you select what gives you more of the feelings you are looking for.

If you believe that you will be worse off for watching something, reading something, or attending an event, drop it. It may sound obvious, but many of us persist or do it unconsciously out of habit. Instead of spending time and energy on news that causes you stress, flip it.

Spend time on inspiring books and movies, create memories with your loved ones, take up a cool new hobby or activity, or do something that fills you with feel-good hormones.

Move your body and fill your glass

I don't know about you, but if I haven't moved much physically for a few days, I feel tensions build up and I am more easily impacted by stressful events. I feel less calm inside, small things can trigger me more easily, and finding solutions to some of life's challenges becomes a challenge in itself.

Kelly McGonigal, Ph.D., author of *The Joy of Movement,* explains it this way: "On days when people exercise, stressful things take less of a toll on their well-being. You're more resilient because of how movement makes you feel about yourself and your capacity to handle challenges. Not only that, regular exercise changes your brain over time and maintains brain health. Studies show that after six weeks of activity, we see functional and structural changes in the brain's reward system that are similar to what you see from the most advanced treatments for depression. The result is that people feel more motivated and are better able to experience joy and happiness in everyday life. There are also changes in the systems of the brain that help regulate emotions and keep stress in check. So after weeks of regular activity, you've built a more resilient brain that will help you keep calm in a crisis."

On the mornings during the week when I jump on my cross trainer for 20 minutes, I feel that I have completely destressed my body and cleared my mind for what's coming up during the day.

I feel so much more relaxed and able to handle what otherwise would have created higher levels of mental and physical stress. This self-awareness has boosted my motivation and frequency for doing this and other forms of exercise before starting my day.

McGonigal goes on to clarify: "The exercise doesn't have to be hard. Moving your body in any way, with any degree of intensity, can do it. That said, many of the resulting benefits are amplified by intensity."

I noticed that when I stretch too much or push too hard, then I am significantly lower on vital energy the next day. Observing how you feel during and after exercising, and adjusting according to what your aims are, will help reap the rewards while avoiding any unwanted effects. Tune into how your body feels, go with the exercise type and intensity that works best for you, change it up for variety, build it into your agenda, and keep topping up your glass.

Do what gives you energy

You may be thinking that this seems to be very selfish, all of this focusing on yourself, especially if you have a family with kids. Let's reframe that thought for a moment. When you feel that your glass is empty, so to speak, how well are you able to be there for someone else? When you're really feeling the stress and pressure of the events of your day or your life, how much can you really do for others?

What do you do that gives you energy and that feels good? And how often do you do it? Friends and clients have cited the following ways of getting their energy to a good place: spending time cuddling or playing with their pet, light exercise, reading a great book over a cup of tea, meditating to relaxing music, tidying up their place, making and sharing a healthy meal, and even shopping for something cool or unique.

For me, it depends on where I am and how much time I have available. On the weekend, if I'm home, I go for a solo hike in the vineyards for up to two hours. I find that the combination of alone time, combined with movement, has a huge grounding effect on my mood and emotions. As well as dissipating stress, it also gives me the opportunity to step back and have a fresh perspective on whatever's going on at that moment in my life. It opens up my mind to think of new options, ideas, and solutions.

How about you? What really helps you feel better? What do certain activities do for you, either mentally, physically, or emotionally? Focus for a moment on how you feel afterward, on how they change your state in a positive, meaningful way.

Now think of how often you do them and how often you would like to do them. Then think of the possibilities you have in your day or your week where you could plug these into your agenda. Then just go make them happen. I know time is the reason we all give for not doing more of this, but if you make it a priority, you'll find the time. One way that comes to mind is to start to say no to certain things that are not a priority for you. I remember a powerful message from a time-management class that stands out for me: When you say "yes" to something that takes your time, you are automatically saying "no" to everything else you could do at that same moment.

Activity: Awareness of the Benefits

Let's increase your level of self-awareness around what certain activities do for your energy and moods and how to leverage them further.

Think about the activities in your week that typically enhance your mood. Do they create and let a physical vibrancy in your body, give you a temporary brain break from your situation or stress, make you feel like you can conquer the world, or at least any challenge life throws your way?

Capture in the table below what those activities are for you.

What can you do to get the most from their benefits? What can you do to use the state these activities have created in you to advance in other ways? And if it's just to feel relaxed or zen afterwards, that's perfectly OK.

You could also use that state to visualize all the things you love about yourself, decide and take the first step on what will create a positive outcome in your week, or access the higher version of yourself to find a more empowering story around a current life challenge you're facing. To ensure it's clear, I've given an example below.

My example…

Walking in nature

Every couple of weeks

A gentle way of increasing my heart rate

Clean, fresh air

Time for myself to focus on what I can feel grateful for

Refreshed, invigorated

A mild physical fatigue

Being pulled towards taking actions I thought of during my walk

May be helpful to create a list on my phone of what I'd like to focus on, or find solutions for, during my next walks.

While walking, think of what I feel grateful for or on actions I can take for some of life's challenges and goals.

Include mindful walking as part of it.

Once per week

Every Sunday morning

OK, over to you…

Activity

How often I do it

What I get from it

How I feel afterwards

Keep Your Glass Topped Up

Anything I should do differently

How I can use it (even more)

How often I am doing it from now on

When I am now going to include this in my schedule

Keep getting better at something

Keeping your glass topped up also means feeling good about yourself as well as about your life. If you are stagnating, it's challenging to then feel good about where you are and how your life's going.

What's the one thing you would like to do or to get better at? Play classical guitar, learn to speak whatever language appeals to you most, handstand with no support, dance tango, run a marathon, become a psychologist…?

Putting your energy into something and seeing the progress you're making along the way will enhance your self-image and self-esteem. This helps to do what the American Psychological Association terms nurturing a positive view of yourself. And it fills your glass with the good stuff.

Turn your thoughts to what you are grateful for

Back to gratitude again, as it's a huge glass filler and so easy to do as a habit. Practice it regularly, and your glass will never be empty.

Check in with yourself and notice, day by day, how full or empty your glass is. Then schedule your day to include whatever works best for you to top it up and reduce what's draining it.

With your glass topped up now, let's look next at what to do when life knocks it over.

CHAPTER 11

When You're in the Eye of the Storm ...

"Where there is light, there must be shadow,
where there is shadow there must be light.
There is no shadow without light
and no light without shadow."
— Haruki Murakami

When you think about it, the weather has a lot of parallels with life.

There is a rainbow behind many storms, both weather storms and life storms...

Most of the time, we don't get to even notice the rainbow because we're too busy complaining about the rain, temporarily blinded to what's good and simply feeling like we're in the eye of the storm. To see that rainbow, you may need to step back, lift your head up, and look at the storm from another perspective.

In a way, what we'll do in this chapter is to help you see that beautiful rainbow in your storm.

When you're on a roll, things seem so easy, almost effortless. It's like when you have the wind at your back, gently pushing you forward. With that momentum, you feel as though you're capable of almost anything. You're getting great work completed, you're actively taking care of your body, you're reading great books, and have a beautiful energy in your relationships and your life. Your life is "in the flow," so to speak.

Then comes a storm, at times sudden, at times expected, sometimes a minor one, and occasionally a hurricane.

When it seems like things can't get any worse, or any more difficult, the rain pours down, accompanied by a now-gale-force wind that feels like it's pushing you backwards.

That's the way life operates. Events can happen at any time and can take something or someone away from you. Perhaps it's a sudden accident, or a new boss with whom you can't get along, or you have a relationship that is ending, or your job is being outsourced. Whatever it may be, you feel like your life is under a dark cloud and it's pouring rain on you.

Let's see how we can swing that around and learn to dance in the rain instead. Let's also help those clouds dissipate, shall we?

Let's get in a stronger state.

You may be asking me, "What do you mean, stronger state? With the way my life is right now, I feel like crap. I'm sitting here watching Netflix, eating some chocolate, and taking a break from what's going on."

By the way, if you've binge watched a series, I completely get it. I do it too on occasion. It's one way to relax and unwind. Not saying it's the best way, but hey, sometimes it feels like that's just what the doctor ordered. Spending hours or a few evenings like this can be just what you need at particular moments. At the same time, doing it a certain way may just zap your energy further, which isn't the best idea. The last time I did this, I learned my lesson. Watching a series starring Kiefer Sutherland for a couple of nights straight until the early hours of the morning seemed like a good idea at the time. It took my focus away from stuff that I didn't feel like thinking about. I remember a few hours in, around 2:00 a.m., I was feeling peckish. So I heated up a leg of duck, which I had to accompany, of course, with a glass of red to help it go down. Happy with my idea, I sat back down, enjoying my late-night snack, for another hour or two, as the story was so compelling. The default mode on Netflix is cleverly designed so as one episode ends, the next one begins, with no action needed from your side. Fortunately for me, it was a Friday night. Let's just say my head didn't feel like it was on the outside of my body the next morning. It felt as though it had been put somewhere that doesn't often see the sunlight.

If that's your mood or mode right now, I fully understand. At the same time, if you're reading this, despite feeling like crap, it means some part of you wants more. Let's focus on that part of you.

Here's a quick exercise that I would like for you to do.

Sit on a chair or sofa. Now slouch over, put your head down, and make sure your breath is shallow and your shoulders curved inwards.

How do you feel now? Maybe put your head in your hands for full effect. Feel all optimistic, dynamic, and excited about your life? Or does your physical and emotional energy feel low? I would bet it's the latter.

OK, let's change it up. Now stand up. Stand tall with your shoulders back, chest out, your head up, and your eyes looking forward. Breathe from your belly with nice deep breaths. To bring it up a level, put a big smile on your face. Feel the difference?

Next, go put on your favorite uplifting song. Something with a dance rhythm or with powerful lyrics or both. Turn up that volume, put on your headset if need be, and jump around, sing, or dance. Let yourself go. Feel the song, the music, and move along with it.

Now how are you feeling? Better, right?!!

In fact, a recent review in the *World Journal of Psychiatry* found that music therapy can be an effective treatment for mood disorders. After reviewing 25 trials, the researchers concluded that music is a valid therapy to potentially reduce depression and anxiety, as well as improve mood, self-esteem, and quality of life. Another study in the *Journal of Positive Psychology* found that people who listened to upbeat music could improve their moods and boost their happiness in just two weeks.

Playing a high-energy tune, just as I sit on the edge of my bed upon waking, has helped me on numerous occasions to flip my low-energy lethargic state into one where the energy starts to flow. Often being in the center of a tough situation can create this lethargy in the morning. Maybe you didn't sleep well, pondering over things in your mind during the night, or maybe it's just tough to get up and face the reality that your night's sleep has given you a temporary vacation from. Either way, I find this technique works a treat.

Now that you're in a more dynamic state of energy, do whichever of the strategies below that you feel will be most helpful right now.

Identify what's worked for you in the past

If something has worked for you to get you through one of life's tougher challenges in the past, chances are high that it may also serve you this time around. The fact that you are here today is proof that you are a resilient human being. I want to help you become more aware of the resilience that you've demonstrated in the past, what worked best for you, how incredibly strong you are when you need to be, and see the challenge from another angle. An example from my life is immersing myself in a project. The project I'm referring to is returning to study in the evening with an old friend and completing my first master's degree, in parallel to working full time by day. This was a purposeful distraction and had the added benefit of advancing at least one area of my life, which brought me to a better place.

Activity: Awareness of What's Worked for You

If you reflect on the last 5 to 10 years of your life, what challenges have you encountered? Write them here...

Write down how you were able to get from a negative state back to positive energy? (How did your thought process give you leverage on yourself? What friends did you reach out to and why? What activities did you do? What did you focus on?)

What is at least one positive thing that you can see now, that you couldn't see at the time, about going through any of those challenges?

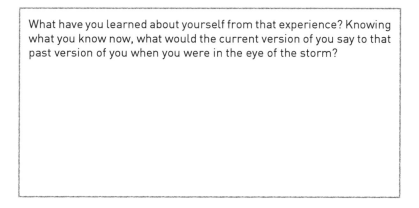

What have you learned about yourself from that experience? Knowing what you know now, what would the current version of you say to that past version of you when you were in the eye of the storm?

Lastly, fast forward to the last days of your life, when you've acquired a lifetime of wisdom. What advice would this kind, optimistic, empathic sage give the you of today about the challenge you're going through?

Discuss with hand-picked friend(s)

It's important to connect with, and accept help and support from, empathetic friends during difficult times. For me, one person I call when I need to air the details of something that's bothering me is my friend Audrey. If I rant a little about some unpleasant situation happening in my life and how bad it seems, she'll give it to me as she sees it. Not how I want her to see it.

She'll then help me focus on either seeing what part I may have played in causing the event or expose the true severity of the situation, which is often less than what I initially portrayed. This takes me completely out of victim mode and helps me see what I can do next, or next time this occurs. I literally feel a difference in how I perceive the situation and am open and ready to take it on from another angle.

Ever discussed bad news with a friend, for them to over-exaggerate the severity of it in their response, and you end up feeling worse for the conversation? It could go something like this...

"I had such a horrible afternoon. My manager seemed to contradict every opinion I gave on our team project."

"That's dreadful. What a jerk your boss must be to do that to you in front of the others! Is he always like that? You shouldn't accept being treated like that. If it was me, I'd look for another job."

They bring the conversation to verbal bashing whoever "caused" the situation and then tell you how you should react in consequence. Some typical comments from this friend could sound like...

"That bastard! And you just let him say that to you..."

"If I were you, I would..."

They mean well, as they care for you, but the outcome isn't what you need. That is, you may feel stupid having "let that happen" and you increase your focus on the negative aspects of the event.

What type of friend should you contact in moments of need then? How about one that will be neutral, unbiased, and tell you what they see or hear, even though it may not be what you want to hear at first. They choose not to take a shortcut in agreeing with you, telling you what you want to hear, and joining your pity party. Instead, they help you understand the role you possibly played leading up to this situation and help you feel empowered to either resolve it or to move on.

Often, when your role in whatever happened is clearer, you stop feeling like a victim, you see it differently, and fresh ideas on how to approach it emerge to you.

In the above example, they may say something like, "That sounds tough." Then they follow that with, "What do you think caused him to react that way?" Then they move on to, "What can you do next for you both to better understand each other's positions and move forward in a way that works for each of you?"

How about you? To whom do you normally go and divulge your hurt to? How do they act? What's the typical reaction? When the conversation ends, do you feel empowered?

If yes, how about thanking them with a hug or a gift?

If you feel worse after the conversation with them, how about picking a different friend next time?

If you're in need of such a chat right now, go connect with that right person. Maybe start with what you appreciate about their perspective and approach and ask if they have a few minutes to help you see things in a more empowering manner.

If it's always the same person, I encourage you, when your energy is in a better place, to balance out these intense conversations with some upbeat conversation or activity with them. Tell them, for example, you realize that your recent conversations were quite heavy due to your situation and that you'd like to break that pattern with a happier chat or doing some cool activity together. If you are also being that friend for them in their moment of need, that's really beautiful. Life is about balance, and so too are our relationships.

Stop focusing on loss

It was mid-summer in France, and I was cycling to the city center. There were too many people walking on the sidewalk, so I decided to follow a tramline to continue cycling. One minute, I was soaking up the ambience created by a mix of tourists and locals under a late afternoon sun. Next minute, I was facedown, sprawled across the tram lines, wondering what happened. Of course, I know it's not a good idea to cycle parallel to a tramline and I had just been reminded why.

One short moment of inattention, and the front wheel of my bike slipped into the slot between the steel tracks. Feeling something was wrong, I instinctively turned the handlebars without thinking. The bike came to a sudden stop, and I flew through the air under the surprised gaze of a terrace full of aperitif drinkers at a nearby bar.

Back on my feet with the help of some sympathetic and caring bypassers, I dusted myself off, uncertain as to what damage I had done. I could just about hold the bike steady with one painful hand grip; the other wouldn't allow me to touch anything with it.

The result was five weeks of having both arms from the thumb to the elbow in resin immobilizing casts. The prognosis was a fractured bone around the base of my right thumb and ligament damage on both wrists.

And this in mid-summer heat, a couple of weeks before a planned vacation on the coast. Vacation was canceled, obviously I couldn't drive my car, and working on my keyboard was impossible, so I had to call the office and let them know. Possibly the most frustrating was attempting to eat with cutlery due to the pain and sudden lack of dexterity. I empathize with elderly folk who, with a trembling hand, try their best at feeding themselves without any collateral damage to items of clothing or to their pride. This was precisely the experience I had while sitting in a restaurant, finding it almost impossible to reach my mouth with a fork balanced between my arm cast and one finger. Luckily, my less-used left hand had just a little more dexterity, due to a less restrictive cast.

From the moment I was leaving the hand clinic with both arms immobilized, seeing the OMG look on my then-partner's face, I could feel myself go into a self-pitying state. You know, into that zone where you feel sorry for yourself and ask what you did to merit such incapacitation and downright bad luck. *How could I have been so stupid? I should have known better!*

I was in that place where my energy, as well as any plans made for the upcoming months, suddenly evaporated, being replaced by negative, self-pitying thoughts. Thinking of all the things that wouldn't be possible. The vacation missed, the sudden imposed need to stop most physical activity, holding hands, cooking dinner or even opening a bottle of water, cycling through the countryside, and most of life's pleasurable moments. Ever tried having an intimate moment with someone without using your hands?

How could I snap out of this self-pity mode?

145

I had a realization. I was focusing on what I had lost, and not what I still had and still could do. All I damaged were my wrists. I did not knock my head and therefore avoided possible severe injury. You see, I wasn't wearing a helmet. Yes, I know, it was imprudent for sure. I especially know now. And when I looked in the mirror upon getting home, I had oil marks around my left temple from the tram line. My head had touched the ground upon falling but did not hit the ground with any impact. I was so lucky.

That was it. That was a huge positive. "It's only my wrists, and they'll recover." The rest of me was fine. This one distinction was a big one. It got me through the duration of the cast-wearing weeks, and the long recovery.

Feeling like I was rather lucky now, I asked myself another question. "What can I still do?"

Well, I couldn't type on my PC keyboard, so in order to stay in touch with the office, I started to use the Dictaphone function on my iPhone to write and reply to mails.

"What else can I do?"

Well, I wanted to finish this book for a while now but never had the time, or never took the time, rather. Now I had time.

I took out the MacBook that I'd bought on an impulse when I had first started the book, I checked on YouTube how the dictation function worked, and I was off.

If you focus on the past or what's missing from your life, or what you used to have and you don't have any more, it'll drive your stress levels up and may prevent you from advancing and getting back to a positive energy state.

Get yourself in a strong positive state and focus on what you still have.

Activity: A Focus on What's Still in Your Life

You may be going through a rough patch right now, but what is it that you still have or that you still can do that you are grateful for?

So that your brain really understands this, be as specific as possible in what you write down. Also, start each line with the word "I" and write in a positive tone.

For additional bonus points, read back through your list, close your eyes, and see each one of these, while truly feeling appreciative for what you still have and still can do.

I can (still)...	I still have...

Let me show you what I had after my accident…

I can (still) …	I (still) have …

I can write using the Dictaphone function	My beautiful daughters

I can do exercises without using my hands…stretching, abs, walking	A restaurant in front of my house where I can order a meal, as I can't cook

I can use this time to reflect on what and who are important in my life	My mental faculties, as I was so lucky not to have a head injury

Direct your energy to what you can change or influence

What was my first instinct when my parents separated a few years ago? You guessed it—try to get them to reconcile and to stay together. After all, they were together for almost 50 years. I thought I could influence how they both thought, felt, and behaved. What was the result? Frustration and me losing focus on other areas of my life. I was trying to do the impossible, trying to change others. It felt like trying to ski uphill, and worse, it was like I kept falling down and hurting myself with each step. Then I had my eureka moment. Stop trying to change what's outside of my control and start focusing on what I can have a more substantial influence on, the family. I mean doing what I can to keep everyone on talking terms with one another. I can't control that, but I can influence it.

Think for a moment of a challenge you have right now or have had recently. What is it you are focused on? Where are you putting your energy? If it's nothing you can really change or influence, then ask yourself if you're wasting your precious time and energy, with little or no hope of having an impact.

If that's the case, then flip it. Figure out what you can influence and where you can have an impact. Then change your approach and focus on this. If you're not getting the result you want, a different strategy will lead to a different result. If the challenge feels too big to manage, break it down into bite-size pieces that you can influence and move towards taking action on them. Accept that which cannot be changed and focus on that which you can have an influence on.

Find the diamond in the mud

What to do if you've just been knocked over by one of life's challenges?

Let's go back to the metaphor of a random life storm. What happens in a storm? It rains, right? In fact, it doesn't just rain; it pours. So much water is pouring down that it becomes hard to see in front of you. You stumble upon a large old oak tree and take shelter from the wind. You are not necessarily seeking to advance for the moment but just to get out of the elements and recover somewhat. You feel worn down by the storm and maybe even fall to your knees or sit. All this rain has turned the ground to mud, and here you are kneeling or sitting in the middle of it.

You're not able to see far ahead and are downtrodden by the conditions you're facing. Just when you feel you don't have the energy to get back on your feet and keep going, something catches your eye. It glitters and sparkles, right there in the middle of the mud. You see it. It grabs your full attention, and your eyes zoom into it like the lens of a camera. The closer you zoom, the more the anticipation builds. You feel something inside. Your heartbeat changes, and your facial muscles, which were placid in despair, now start to engage. Your gaze widens, and your eyelids raise up. You move the mud out from around it and carefully examine this beautiful phenomenon you have discovered. You pick it up to distance it from the wet mud. You realize what it is and above all, the value it has for you. It's a diamond. Its value in this unpleasant context has multiplied ten times over. On a typical day, you'd appreciate it, but here in the middle of one of life's tough storms, its beauty, how precious it is, feels like a gift sent from above. It has given you the strength to get back on your feet. You stand up, wipe yourself off, lift your gaze up, and start to advance. You've been through storms in the past. You always got through them, and this is no different. Even if you don't see it yet, soon your days will have the sun shining on you again.

"OK, nice story, Trevor, but I usually don't find diamonds in the mud." I get it, really. Me neither. As you may have guessed, the diamond represents something of beauty that you can appreciate, and even more so during a challenging period. It uplifts you. It gets you to smile, even if just on the inside.

What are some of life's "precious diamonds," then?

Seeing your child smile, a kind word from a friend who calls up to check in on you, the realization that despite this challenge, you still have a beautiful life …

You have also captured some of your diamonds in your gratitude journal if you've created one. As we discussed in Chapter 8, gratitude can be practiced just in the mind and can also be done by writing what you're grateful for into a journal. Here we're seeing another advantage of capturing your gratitude moments in writing. As you read through your journal, in a way, you get to relive some of those moments. This can help fill what may feel, for some people, like a certain emptiness inside, depending how bad your storm feels to you. I want to ensure we capture one last point here. What if you feel right now that it's difficult to find something to be grateful for, and on top of that, when you reread your past gratitude moments in your journal, you feel like, "That was the past. Life was better back then. It'll never be that way again"'? Depending on your storm and current mindset, this is a possible reaction. I've been there a couple of times myself for short periods and I know it's not a nice place to be.

So, how do you get over this right now?

I don't know you, but I'm quite sure that you've experienced joyous moments, loving moments, and fun moments in your life. Some were created by you, and others you had the privilege of being on the receiving end. In the eye of your storm, you may feel that it's not possible to create these moments in your life right now. If so, think of one thing you can do now for someone and do it. Not only will it be a beautiful moment for them; it'll also be one for you and may give you the momentum to create others.

Look at it differently... Ask yourself better questions

You're caught up in a challenging life event, a situation you'd prefer didn't happen. It's now key to take control of your inner voice, to overwrite anything that's working against you. To reprogram and replace what's not helpful. Doing some of what we've described up to now has been preparation for this in a sense. Now is possibly when you'll get the most benefit from pivoting your mind, asking better questions, and answering from your highest self.

Life does have periods where days are not so bright. So, during these darker moments, apart from waiting for them to brighten up, what can we do?

Here's a reminder of the empowering questions from Chapter 9 to help you pivot, to help your brain see the options and possibilities you still have, despite the current challenge.

If it happened to a friend, what would I advise him / her to focus on or to do here? What question would I ask?

What else could this mean?

How can I use this for the greater good?

Avoid things that will peak your stress or anxiety to an even higher level

If possible, it may be best to temporarily avoid people or situations that will stress you even further. That may be a certain friend, family member, or colleague. I'm not suggesting avoiding them completely or cutting them out of your life, but distance yourself if you just know that a conversation with them right now will have you feeling worse off, at a time when you're looking to feel in a better place. If the context is fitting, first allow yourself the space to get into a better place mentally and emotionally. It's not a question of being self-centered; it's a question of knowing your limits and respecting your needs.

If there's a risk of creating any potential unwanted impact by doing so, then estimate what you'll gain versus any likely loss or harm, and make your choice considering both.

Most people are reasonable, and if you explain to them that you need time to get your energy back to a better place, they'll normally understand. How you communicate this can be key, as is the case when discussing any sensitive subject. One way is to do it in a manner where you calmly express why you need this time, adding that you'll be back to them soon, when you'll be more able to be there in whatever way the situation or relationship calls for. In addition to this, let them know that you truly appreciate their understanding.

Do one thing to make today a better day

A talented HR professional recently told me she was close to burnout. Her career was going through a rough patch, and the relationship with her manager deteriorated to a point where even the thought of speaking one to one with him was stressful. She was already using the above strategy and was temporarily avoiding certain colleagues, while keeping an eye on ensuring she wasn't missing anything critical.

We spoke for a while, and apart from reflecting on some questions to reframe her view on her current situation, she agreed she would do one additional thing.

She would ask herself each day, "What can I do today for this to be a good day, or a better day than what I am anticipating?" Note, the question is not: "What can I do to make it a great day or an outstanding day?" The goal is to make the day better than what she imagined it would be like.

If you find yourself in a challenging or stressful position, and need to feel like you're in a better place, make a conscious effort to do something to make each day a good one. Take a step, even a small one, to advance towards an achievable goal, put on relaxing music and meditate for 10 minutes, take a 30-minute break to read your favorite novel, give a friend or colleague a sincere compliment, do something for someone else, or go for a walk or run in nature. Each of us is unique, so reflect on what can make your day better than what you had anticipated and take pleasure in doing it.

It is totally normal to feel sad on occasion and to allow yourself some time immersed in those deep emotions that are not very comfortable. Give yourself the space to not be OK. I believe it's just not a good place to live for a long time, and the techniques here are designed to get yourself back to a good place.

Even so, you may very well feel sadness and regret return from time to time, and that's completely normal. Achieving an important goal is not a straight-line affair, and neither is recovering from a substantial stressful event. Be kind and gentle with yourself. You deserve it.

Focus on what you can change, accept what you can't, connect with someone you know will help you feel better, take small actions every day towards a realistic goal, appreciate the diamonds in the mud, however small they seem, and do something for others.

Important note: It is important to seek the help of a mental health professional, such as a psychologist, if you feel you cannot handle everyday life activities as a result of a trauma or other stressful life experience.

CHAPTER 12

―――――

Bounce Forward ...

"Winning isn't always a victory, and losing isn't always a defeat."
― Doogie Howser

What does resilience actually mean?

The Oxford Dictionary defines it as "the capacity to recover quickly from difficulties." I'd like to add the notion of not just recovering but also becoming stronger or wiser in the process.

A commonly used definition for resilience is simply "the ability to bounce back." A life event has knocked you over, and you get back up on your feet to where you were beforehand. One step back, one step forward.

At times, we may be fine with just getting back to where we were, and at times, not. I would love for you to be able to come out stronger and better in some way after traversing your challenging situations. Life isn't about maintaining the status quo; it's about growing and developing in different ways based on your situation and stage in life.

Taking one step back, or rather, life knocking you back a step, and then advancing two steps is the metaphor for my preferred definition of resilience. That is, the ability to bounce forward. One step back, two steps forward. It's the sensation of bouncing past your initial starting point.

This feels like something to aim for. It can create some forward momentum that propels you to grow and become a better professional, partner, parent, friend, athlete, or simply a better human being.

Lots of us are knocked back two steps due to a painful or unpleasant situation, and then manage to take one step forward into a less unpleasant, though still unpleasant, situation. And that is okay as a temporary place to be. In fact, it's normal for certain setbacks that you live there temporarily until you figure out a way to advance again.

Staying there for a substantial amount of time or even ending up stuck there is the least desirable outcome. Essentially, being stuck in a place where you have more pain than before the challenge occurred.

Long-term sadness and nostalgia are, of course, normal, if, for example, you've lost someone precious from this life. We may live with emotional pain for many years, at times, forever, when a person we cherished has been taken from us. Please understand that I'm not referring to that type of suffering in this analogy, and I feel so much empathy for you if that is where you are in life right now.

The types of situations I'm referring to include events such as a partner breaking up with you, losing your job, receiving harsh feedback from your manager, not making the team for the championship, making a mistake in business, etc.

So how can we bounce forward? Start with some introspection.

Invest time to reflect

You've been caught up in simply getting through the storm, focusing all your energy on getting out the other side and feeling good about your life again. Your life now may feel like it was before the storm hit, or at least close to what it felt like then. One step back, one step forward. How can you now leverage the storm you've just been through to advance another step?

Take a timeout and give yourself the space to reflect. Go wherever gives you an uplifting energy and gently focus your brain on questions such as...

☐ How can you grow from this? or How have you grown from this?
☐ How can you switch on the best version of you to bounce forward, to bounce back stronger?
☐ How can you be a better person as a result of this challenge?
☐ How can you use the challenge or the associated feelings to do something for someone else?

Asking these questions will flip your focus from your pain to your progress.

What if you could really associate life's challenges with being able to turn on and tune into your higher self? What if you could release some of that potential and wisdom you have on standby inside of you? Change your perspective about tough situations by telling yourself that it's an opportunity to tap into your inner strength and wisdom.

Use pain to your advantage...

Do you want pain? For most people in most situations, the answer is a clear no. Pain can come in many forms. It may be sadness, frustration, anger, disappointment, or at times physical pain.

Although not always obvious, pain often has benefits. At this point, you may be saying, "Benefits? Are you crazy? I don't want the benefits if I have to have the pain." However, pain, if it's not extreme physical pain, can help us to be better versions of ourselves. Bear with me while I explain.

Consider this business phenomenon. When one of your customers is unhappy about something you did or didn't do, and then you fix their issue in the right way, studies have shown that they are more loyal to your business than before they ever had the problem in the first place. Now, does that mean that you should create more problems for your customers so that you can have happier customers by putting a lot of energy and the right approach to fixing the problems? No, this wouldn't be an advisable business strategy for reasons we won't get into here. The point being, you don't want unhappy customers (painful for you), but if you do have one, with the right strategy, you can leverage this (painful situation) to your advantage and improve your business (benefit for you).

It's the same thing with our personal, emotional pain. We can use it to create something better. Pain can drive us to change how we eat, to look for a new job, to find someone we're more compatible with, or to quit smoking. Even the pain associated with boredom can move us out of our comfort zone to create a more interesting day or a more interesting life.

If you are experiencing some form of pain right now, be it physical or emotional, I welcome you to complete the next activity.

Activity: Visualization to Leverage Your Pain

Sit somewhere you can be calm and close your eyes.

Take several deep breaths through your nose with a longer exhale through your mouth. You are activating the calming system of the body and will start to feel more relaxed.

Sit strong and tune into your higher you. The version of you who has succeeded through all of life's challenges to get to where you are now. The you who has nearly limitless potential.

From this state say, "I am the master of my body and feelings. This pain is just a tool that I am, as of now, using to improve life in some way, for myself and others."

Feel this power inside of you and ask yourself...

"How can my pain best serve me to create something good for myself and for others?"

As soon as you've found an answer, and it feels right for you, make the decision that you will use your pain as leverage for whatever action you've identified.

Visualize yourself taking that action. See and feel the impact this has on you, and on whomever else it benefits.

Gently come back to your breath and feel the energy you've created pulling you forward towards making it happen in reality. Capture your thoughts in your journal and then go make it happen.

You can also find the guided version at www.trevorlynch.net

Visualize your outcome

Let's use this super effective tool once again. My question for you is, how do you want it to look as you come out the other side of the storm? Want to be back to how you were before it hit, or an even better version of you? Maybe you want to be happy, or happier, in a new job or new relationship. It may be that you want to feel vibrant and upbeat again in your daily life.

See yourself at a future point in time, when you've come through this challenging even and come out the other side. Picture yourself on the other side of the storm as a resilient, stronger version of yourself who has adapted as the situation required.

Feel how it feels to have succeeded through it. Visualize how your days are, how you interact with others, how your newly found energy feels in your body, and see a smile on your face again. Tune into the empowering beliefs about yourself and the resilience you can call on when needed.

From this place, listen to and take in the message from that future version of you before finishing by coming back to your breath and back to your day.

Repeat as often as you wish and capture your thoughts in your journal so you can refer back to them when you could do with a positive reminder of how your life will be soon.

Life is not meant to be lived in the status quo. When it knocks you back, figure out how you can grow, despite the challenge, or even thanks to the challenge. I agree that I am giving a simplistic view here and that it can be, or appear, much more complex, depending on the severity of the challenge and pain. At the same time, focusing on the pain will amplify it further in your mind. Focusing on how you want your life to be can pull you in that direction, towards that vision. One painful step back, two growth steps forward.

PART 3

SO WHAT NEXT?

CHAPTER 13

━━━━━━

What to Focus on Next ...
With a Strategic Life Break

"The future depends on what you do today."
— Mahatma Gandhi

One of my favorite moments is sitting in a cafe where the ambiance
is relaxed and the decor has a cozy, modern feel to it. I'm sipping on
herbal tea, often an invigorating blend containing ginger and something to round its spicy edge like cinnamon.

I have a table to myself, with more than enough space for a
notebook, my MacBook, and an empty stretch on the countertop to
allow me to maneuver a Bluetooth mouse.

I have some form of relaxing instrumental music playing through
my headset to distance my mind from the rumbling noise of a cafe
full of chatter.

I just sit there with a soft, focused gaze and reflect on my life.
Where am I at in each area of life that's important to me? What's
going on that's impacting it in one direction or another? What have
I been focusing on recently, and what's been the result? What have I

been neglecting, and what's the outcome of that inattention? What should I pay more attention to, and what should I continue?

It's a moment where I step off this crazy hamster wheel of constantly checking emails, juggling work priorities, coordinating last-minute requests, grocery shopping, paying bills, or running errands. Depending on where you are on the journey of life, this list for you may also include chaperoning your kids around to their various activities and interests that they grow from and enjoy.

Taking a step back from your day-to-day routine and looking at your life objectively will shine a light on how good certain areas are and how others could do with some focus or change of approach. Chances are that many areas are performing well and give you a feel-good sentiment about your life, and others may cause you to cringe when you look at them. At times in the past, when I've reflected on parts of my life that weren't going so well, I've avoided going deep due to wanting to avoid cringing and feeling frustration or disappointment with myself. Cringing doesn't sound very appealing, I know, but it's better to cringe now than to cry later. It's about stepping back and taking a photograph of what your life looks like at a particular point in time, reflecting on what you're noticing, both on paper and inside of you, and deciding what to focus on going forward.

How valuable would it be for you, your life, and your level of fulfilment, to take even 30 minutes every few months to do this? How would it benefit you, and those around you, if you took that step off the hamster wheel to enable certain realizations? To enable you to correct the course of your romantic relationship, or the state of your finances, or your physical condition. To allow yourself to plan for a life that's closer to your dreams.

What are you doing with your battery life?

A friend of mine called me one day and asked an interesting question, which led to an interesting conversation. "I was thinking, imagine if you were an iPhone, how much battery life would you have left?"

The conversation continued by underlining that a big difference between us and an iPhone is that we don't have a charger. So, positioning myself as an iPhone with no charger, how much battery life could be left? We went on discussing the average life spans right now according to the latest statistics, and I estimated that I had maybe 40 percent, if all went well. And obviously, like an iPhone, one could die from one day to the next from an accident or some other fault.

If you are in your twenties or thirties, and you're reading this, then you may not yet realize the speed at which life goes by. It's been my experience that this nonchalance of youth concerning our relationship with time, or seeing it as a precious resource, comes to an end either in or around our forties, or as we experience our kids' birthdays, or we see our parents celebrate a big milestone birthday. Regardless of your level of battery life left, it's useful to step back from the day-to-day hustle and take stock. Certain realizations and actions at almost any age can make such a difference to how you live your life, your level of joy and fulfilment, and the impact you have on others. This is what this chapter is focused on.

Strategic Life Break

Let's talk about this activity I call a "strategic life break." It can be done anywhere that feels right for you, so long as you're somewhere where the daily demands of life are not distracting you. A break from emails, social media, and from unwanted interruptions. As I said above, one of my favorite places to do this is in a cafe, though I've been known to take an annual trip to Nice and reflect on my life over an ice-cold glass of rosé while being immersed in the Mediterranean atmosphere.

A previous director I worked for retreats to the mountains twice a year. His focus is mainly oriented on his professional life. He ponders such questions as: What had we planned for the past six months? What did we achieve? Did we hit our goals? What was instrumental to that success? What did we miss? What caused us to not yet reach our expected level? How do we course correct? What's the plan for the next six months? What do we need to do to make that happen?

It's completely your choice whether to focus on your personal life, your professional context, or a combination of both. It's up to each of us to also be aware of what will work for our situation and our personality. For some, it's a weekend away on the coast, somewhere warm, and for others, it's a stolen hour or two sitting on a cafe terrace. Go wherever works for you, for as long as you feel is needed or is possible.

Your life in perspective

With that decided, how can you structure your reflection? I'm going to walk us through one way using a tool that's designed for that purpose, called "The Wheel of Life."

The Wheel of Life, also known as the life balance wheel, is a visual tool used to assess and understand how balanced your life currently is. Using this tool, you map out the areas of your life on a circle that resembles the spokes of a wheel, which is the reasoning for its name. The original concept of The Wheel of Life is attributed to Paul J. Meyer, who founded the Success Motivation® Institute in 1960.

Before I walk you through the steps, let me show you an example. When you do this for your life, you get to choose the categories you wish to focus on and how to word them so they have the most meaning for you.

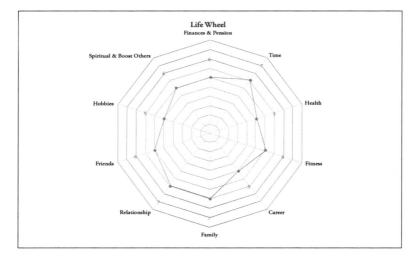

It's quite easy. Now that you've seen an example of a completed life wheel, just follow the steps below to create yours...

Go to www.trevorlynch.net and download a free worksheet for this exercise.

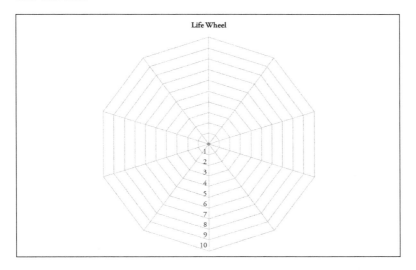

Life Wheel

1. On the outside of the chart, fill in the names for the areas of life that are most important for you.
2. Rate yourself on a scale of 1 to 10 for each area (10 meaning "It couldn't be better"; 1 meaning "I don't think it could be any worse"; and then everything in between)
3. Decide where you feel you want to give more priority or focus right now by placing an 'x' next to the category name.
4. On the wheel, write down a rating that you want to bring these priority areas to. Feel free to be optimistic while still being realistic about what's possible in the next few months.
5. Allow yourself a moment to feel great about certain areas, then decide what to do in order to better some of the others

Note: In the editable version at www.trevorlynch.net you can comment on the reason you rated each category as you did, so as to remind yourself of the logic you used when you next look at your chart.

I remember doing this exercise a few years ago. After I had filled in the ratings, I looked at the graph. What I felt was a mixture of shock and overwhelm. The ratings on many of the areas were low, and I felt like it would be too much to take on, to try to increase so many of them at once.

If this is you currently, my first piece of advice is to go easy on yourself. Like the seasons, life goes in cycles. I suggest selecting one or two areas that you would benefit most from boosting right now. In the exercise below, write down and plan what you can and will do over the coming days and weeks. This will help you to focus and advance step by step.

When you've decided on what you will do this week, stop reading, pick one action, and do it today, or at least plan it in your calendar. Create some momentum. Often the first step is the hardest to take, and when you've taken it, the feel-good hormones will help you move to your next action, and your next…

If you feel you can jump 3, 4, or 5 points quite easily, then by all means, knock yourself out and go for it, but be OK with starting small. From experience, aiming to go from a 6 to a 10 is quite a challenge. Remember, the aim is not to have the perfect relationship or financial situation right away. Instead, the aim is to keep advancing, creating balance, feeling a sense of achievement, and feeling good, or better, about yourself and your life.

Now that your chart is completed, go ahead and fill in the following.

The areas I feel great about and why

What to Focus on Next ... With a Strategic Life Break

What Life area(s) I'm excited about improving right now:

1.
2.
3.

What I'll do to bring it or them to the next level:

What date I will set for myself to have achieved this by:
(Plan this in your calendar to maximize your chances of following through.)

What I'll do this week to advance on my action(s):

Who will hold me accountable and offer guidance as needed:

P.S. You could include this in your next visualization, helping yourself to see it as done.

When you next review your wheel, be it in one month or three months, chances are it will have changed. Life is forever evolving. Even if you do nothing in some areas, life's randomly occurring events will change the game for you. That's just how it is. When I started this activity a few years back, I thought my aim, and a realistic aim at that, was to bring each area to a 9 or a 10 rating. I was fooling myself. Too many things occurred, and there were so many things to focus on for me to achieve that. And, of course, what one person calls a 10, someone else rates a 6. It's all relative. I select the area, or few areas, of life that make the most sense to put my energy into right now, and I spend the next month mainly focusing on those. It doesn't mean I completely neglect the others; my priority areas just stand out more on my mental radar, and my actions are mainly planned around them.

An interesting addition to your agenda

You've completed your life wheel, decided on your focus areas, and created your action plan. What's next? Apart from taking the actions, the last step in the process is to review and update your ratings regularly. I recommend anything from every one to six months. Pick the duration that's the sweet spot for your personality and lifestyle. When deciding the ideal frequency for you, consider a time gap that's short enough to enable you to keep the momentum and long enough between cycles for you to take certain actions and observe their impacts. For the process to be effective, I wouldn't let more than six months go by before reviewing and updating your Life Wheel.

For the first and future review cycles, I suggest you start with reflecting on the following points and add any additional reflection points or questions that you find valuable.

Since my last strategic life break...

What I have progressed on includes...

What I have learned is...

What have I learned about myself is...

How will I use what I learned to optimize my approach in the next cycle?

Then, celebrate where you are as well as the areas you feel good about, and update your Life Wheel and action plan.

Life goes by so fast. Before realizing it, you may have concentrated so much on certain areas that you didn't notice the areas you were neglecting. It's completely normal. Course correct by taking a time out to look at the bigger picture. Celebrate what's going well and make a decision as to what is priority for you at this moment. Schedule your next timeout and repeat the cycle, including the awareness-enhancing observation points above.

Have fun with this, share with your partner or friends as you wish, and I'd love to hear from you on your insights and progress. (My contact details appear at the end of Chapter 15.)

CHAPTER 14

Make a Difference

"The smallest deed is better than the greatest intention."
— John Burroughs

It was a midsummer Saturday night in Paris. We had booked a few nights in a trendy 4-star hotel at the edge of the Marais district, a location with quirky boutiques and cobblestone streets.

At 3:45 in the morning, I awoke with a thirst, a sudden need for hydration before falling back to sleep. In the dimly lit room, I reached for the Evian water bottle on the bedside locker and drank a few mouthfuls. As soon as I parted the bottle from my lips, I realized it wasn't water.

It tasted like a cleaning product.

Half asleep and now startled at the event that just occurred, I awakened my then girlfriend and asked that she smell the top of the open bottle and tell me what it was. She wasn't fully awake and was confused. I explained what had happened, and she smelled the top of the open bottle. She confirmed it was surely some form of cleaning product, and definitely not water!

A form of panic came over me. I walked toward the hotel room door, and it felt like I almost froze just before reaching it. I was completely absorbed in my thoughts. All my thoughts were focused on what was happening inside of me. "Is this it? Should I call my daughters and say goodbye? What if I survive this? I'd just be frightening them for little or no reason."

My brain was then flooded with questions. *If I die, will my daughters and parents be okay? Did I leave my daughters with nice memories? Did I give them the right messages about life? Did I tell them how much I loved them, and what I loved about them?*

I was brought back to the task at hand with a request from the other side of our hotel room. "Chéri, can you go ask at the reception what exactly the liquid was in that water bottle, which the hotel staff had surely left in the room? I have the 24/7 anti-poison hotline person on the phone. They need this information in order to give you the right guidance."

Long story short... After 12 hours in Accident & Emergency in a Paris hospital and four weeks with internal burns in my throat and esophagus, I'm still here to tell the tale. What was in the bottle was a transparent, multi-surface cleaning liquid that the cleaning person from the hotel had transferred from a larger container to a small Evian water bottle and had forgotten it in our room. I was so incredibly lucky that it didn't burn completely through the fragile tissue in my throat.

When we look back...

I would have thought that when faced with a life-threatening situation, I would most certainly focus on the decisions I had made at certain moments in life. To stay or to move on, to live in one place or another, to have had the courage to go for certain goals or not. Maybe I would focus on the relationships I stayed in for too long or those I should have given more effort to. Or on the career I had or could have had. Or on what I did or didn't do in my life. In short, I thought I would have focused on the life I had lived. Hoping and knowing my daughters would be well is, of course, part of that life reflection, a tremendously important part. However, on this day, when I thought it would be the end for me within a few minutes, that's all I was thinking about. Nothing else seemed to matter to me, except my "babies."

Life doesn't always lead us to our final day with advance notice, to allow us to ponder and give us the time to do and say what's really important for those we care about.

If your day was to come suddenly, unexpectedly, how content would you be, not just with the life you have lived but with the legacy you'd leave behind for those you love?

It's not something I had thought about until that fateful night in Paris.

On an intellectual level, I know what's important when our day comes is not just about how we lived, what we achieved, the career we had, or the lifestyle we enabled for ourselves and our families. For sure, that's a big part of it. Reaching as much of the potential we've been blessed with is part of what we're here to do. Contributing to others is surely as, or even more, meaningful.

Improving others' lives, in even a miniscule way, by a gesture, a smile, or offering a kind word to lift their spirits, is part of what makes humankind so human. It's about making the lives of those you love, those you come into contact with, and those you'll never get to meet better on some level, better because you lived and what you did during your life.

This is not the absolute truth of how it is, but it's what I believe, and the near-death experience implanted this much more profoundly than just on an intellectual level.

The focus of this book up to this point has been on how you can be a better and more resilient version of you, at times when you most need to be. Now, we're going to take that higher version of you and, with your permission, use it also for the greater good.

Pure giving

How often do we tell those we care about what we like, appreciate, admire, and love about them?

I had this experience recently with a good friend of mine, where I called him mid-evening.

"Are you sitting down?" I asked.

"Wow, this sounds serious. Is everything OK?"

"Yes, all is good. Pour yourself a glass and pull up a chair. I'd like to tell you something."

"Okaaay."

It felt strange, but at the same time, it was completely worth the temporary uncomfortable feeling of speaking from my heart, not just my head. Pure giving to someone who merits hearing the positive impact his words, friendship, and advice often had on me. In the professional world, we often use the term "feedback," or "positive feedback," for this, for telling somebody what we appreciate about what they've just done, or how they've been in a certain context.

How about in our personal lives? Do we often take the time and allow ourselves to offer a beautiful moment of appreciation to someone we care about? What I mean is, to take a moment and tell them all the things we really appreciate about them as a person. Think about it for a second or two. Do you do this with your parents, your partner, your friends, your children, your siblings, those who are most important in your life? From what I've seen, we do not, or at least not enough. I know I hadn't done this frequently enough in my own life. We feel that they understand this from how we are with them, that they can read between the lines, but can they really? Wouldn't it be a pity if it's not the case?! And even if it was, wouldn't it be so heartwarming for them to hear it said?

Even if you feel, or believe, someone loves you, isn't it still a heartfelt moment when they say those three words as a kind of affirmation of their feelings? We can even long for it, from our partner, our children, or even from our parents. We know they love us from their actions and at the same time, we may, at certain moments, yearn for the words to come from their lips. They very possibly feel the same. Hearing "I love you" triggers hormones inside of us that warm the heart and ease the mind, a feeling that comes from knowing we are loved, truly loved.

At the same time, what do they love about you? Ever wondered? They may be wondering the same thing. How about taking your expression of love a step further and telling your loved ones what you appreciate about them specifically?

Do it now

What happens when someone's life has ended? If it's someone we cared about, we shed tears and remember all we loved about them, and all that makes us miss them. On the day of their burial, everyone sings the praises of the person who is deceased. The thing is, they can no longer hear it, and so those beautiful, kind words of appreciation may as well go unsaid, as they can no longer make that person feel truly valued. They are gone. The words are vanishing in the wind as they are said, without making that incredible impact that they have the potential for. If only the person they referred to could hear them. Personally, I would prefer to be told those nice things while I'm still here, when they can have the effect of making me feel appreciated, important to those I care about, and loved.

Activity: Your Words to a Loved One

Step 1:
Write a note to a person dear to you, explaining all you appreciate or love about them…big things, little things, how they inspire you, how they make you feel, what you value about them, their quirks, their special qualities, and how them being here makes this world a better place.

Step 2:
This is a challenge for some of us. Offer the gift of those words to that person, in whatever way feels right for you. You can give them a card, or read it to them and offer them the written version for them to keep.

This can be your moment, right now. Put on an emotionally charged song (optional). Come out of your head and allow your heart to express itself. Our heads have been programmed by various cultural influences, such as our family, the education we received, and possibly the company we work for. These cultural influences can be barriers to what we say and how we say it. The true words, the unformatted expressions of deep appreciation, will come from your heart.

This can be a moving, emotional experience. It can cause tears of appreciation to descend your cheeks when your heart opens and expresses itself freely.

The easiest part of this for you may be writing the note of appreciation. Delivering the message can be the challenge. In numerous workshops, when I asked, "How do you feel now about delivering this message?", I've gotten the following reactions…

"I feel anxious about it."

"I feel a little scared, like I'm putting my heart on the line."

"I feel guilty for not having done it before, and at the same time lucky to be given the challenge now."

I recognize the challenge in doing this. At times, I've done it and thought to myself, *Wow, this feels a little weird.* Usually followed by, *but it's deep and beautiful at the same time.* To overcome any uncomfortable feeling, try focusing on the reaction you'll get from the person you're offering this incredible gift to.

If that person has already passed...

When we do a similar activity in one of my workshops, several participants usually express that they think of someone who has passed. Some had the chance to offer such beautiful words to that dear person they had in their lives, and others did not.

If this is something you wished you had done for someone who has passed, and you feel the desire to do it now, please do so. Write your message, then choose how you prefer to offer it to them. It may be going to a beautiful, calm setting of your choice. Possibly by the sea, on a mountainside, in a park early in the morning, or wherever helps you feel calm and thoughtful. Sit, stand, or lie in silence. Imagine spending another moment with them. See them in front of you. See the expression on their face and maybe hear what their voice sounds like one more time. Feel the connection your heart is making with them. Then, when you're ready, read them your message, either silently or with your voice, and imagine the expression on their face. Cherish the moment. What is it telling you? Tell them bye for now and come back to focusing on your surroundings.

Be the one

When you demonstrate this level of appreciation to your family or friends, it's very possible that you're going to be the first to speak on such a deep, heartfelt level.

I remember such an occasion. I was around 15 years old, growing up in Catholic and conservative Ireland.

One Saturday, as I did back then, I went to confession with a couple of friends in a Franciscan church in the city center. I started to ramble off the usual words of commencement, when the priest asked what my first name was. He followed on by asking me if I had ever thrown my arms around my mom and told her that I loved her. *What? In conservative Ireland where no one ever expresses their feelings or emotions? Are you crazy?* My thoughts continued... *No one in our family has ever uttered those words to each other, except, I imagine, my parents to each other.* "No" was the polite response I uttered in return, still taken aback by such a question.

So, the deal was that I should take it upon myself to do this courageous act. From memory, his reason for suggesting it was that she deserved to hear it said out loud.

Gulps!

At the end of an afternoon of hanging with my friends, I walked in the front door of our house and looked for my mom. There I found her, at the stove in the kitchen, preparing an evening meal for the family. I looked at her. She was so engrossed in her work and looked so beautiful. I walked towards her and said the words, "There's no way I can do this. I'm a boy, and no one speaks like that to their parents." I was, of course, speaking to myself, and quickly went to another room to reflect.

And so it was for weeks after. Until, that is, I mustered up the courage one day to give her an unexpected hug and say those words, "I love you Mom!" I vaguely remember the look of real surprise— real, pleasant surprise, I should say—on her tender face.

"I love you too," she responded.

In large corporations, it's a known fact that changing the culture takes time. What I understood from my experience is that the same applies to the culture within a family.

The Oxford Dictionary defines culture as "the customs and beliefs ... way of life ... of a particular country or group." To change the customs and way of life takes time, sometimes generations.

It took many, many years for those three words to be spoken freely within the family, but we got there. All because a 15-year-old boy had been given a challenge by a wise sage and one day found the courage within himself to accept that challenge. The pebble had been dropped in the water. The ripples would touch more and more family members and create a new way of being, a new way of expressing one's feelings for the other family members.

If it's already part of your family culture, then I'm so happy for you. Please continue and consider bringing it to the next level. Let each of your family members know what you appreciate about them. Go from "I love you" to saying what you love about them.

If this is not yet part of your family culture, I invite you to be the first, make the difference, and create that appreciative way of being, way of communicating.

Same with your close friends.

I know it's also tempting to add in a "but I'd really like it if you could change x…"

Nobody is perfect—not you, not I, and not the person you're offering this gift to. I know it, you know it, and they surely know it. They will know that you could have mentioned that thing about them that drives you crazy. But you didn't. You could have and you chose not to. That shows them the purity of this gesture, the maturity of your choice, and the kindness in your heart. What a gift to offer them.

There are so many ways we can make a difference. This chapter has been focused on just one of them. So many people are craving a kind gesture, a meal, a donation, someone to talk to…. Some of them are close to us; others are strangers. The ways each of us can make a difference is endless. By asking ourselves each day, or even each week, what we can do to improve the life of someone else, and then doing it, can make such a difference to the day or the life of another. The choice is ours to make, the actions are ours to take, and the example is ours to give. Life is short, it can often be shorter than what we think, and it's for each of us to decide what we do with our time here.

Live strong, live with sincerity, be courageously vulnerable.

CHAPTER 15

———

Before You Go ...

"It doesn't matter when we start.
It doesn't matter where we start.
All that matters is that we start."
— Simon Sinek

Nobody else on the planet is, or ever will be, exactly like you. No one has your exact gifts, your way of communicating, your way of thinking, or the potential to touch the lives of those around you as you do. Take a look at your "Wow List" right now. This is entirely unique to you.

To release your next level of potential, you just have to step up to it. Use what you've learned here and elsewhere, and bring your self-esteem, your confidence, your achievements, and your impact on others to a level that surpasses what you thought you were capable of.

Remember to be compassionate and kind toward yourself. If things don't go the way you want, or you encounter a difficult moment, give yourself space. Allow yourself to feel those not-so-pleasant emotions. Just don't live there. Don't dwell on them. Use what you've learned here to turn it around and come back stronger and wiser.

When you realize what incredible things you've done and can do, your life can really change for the better. They don't even have to be extraordinary feats. They can be, but they don't have to be. If you have accomplished something you never thought you were capable of, consider it a huge victory, regardless of what it is. If you have made someone else's day, year, or life better in some way, that is awesome. Give yourself permission to acknowledge yourself right now. Recognize that, yes, you have "flaws" and are not perfect, and yes, you are still incredible.

I have one last exercise for you. When you're ready, consider and respond to each of the questions below here or in your journal.

What have I discovered about myself as a result of this journey?

What did I experiment with to succeed my challenge, or bounce forward after a life storm?

What was the outcome?

What will I do next?

One more thing...

If this book has had an impact on you, I encourage you to share what you've learned with those around you—at home, at work, or with a friend who could benefit.

To all of you who have children, nephews, nieces, or grandchildren—when you learn about their worries and concerns, suggest some of what you've learned here to them. Show them how to do it. Let's help them have more self-esteem and confidence in their abilities than we did when we were their age. It will impact their future in such positive and powerful ways. Drop the pebble into the water and observe the ripple effect.

To those of you who lead a team, it's easier to unleash your collective potential, and achieve great things, when each of your team is also equipped to do so individually. I encourage you to walk them through a selection of the exercises and activities outlined in these chapters and share your stories with them. Share your vulnerabilities and what you're doing to overcome challenges, what you're doing to have a more empowering mindset, and what you continue to learn about yourself. Vulnerability and courage are part of what makes a great leader; a leader who is connected to and respected by his or her team.

And that's it! For now...

To all of you who have chosen to take this journey, to be better than you thought possible, I wish you continued strength, self-confidence, and growth. I wish for you an incredible, joyful life, full of opportunities to do amazing things for those you care about, for those you don't even know, and for you.

Always remember: Yes, you freakin' can!

Trevor

P.S. Visit my website at www.trevorlynch.net and follow me on social media to learn about one-to-one coaching options and in-company workshops, as well as programs and events where you can learn and develop further in a live environment with like-minded individuals.

www.linkedin.com/in/trevorlynchprofile

www.facebook.com/TrevorLynchAuthor

www.instagram.com/TrevorLynchAuthor

REFERENCES

Sources are listed in order of appearance.

Chapter 3
Tseng, Julie and Poppenk, Jordan. "Brain meta-state transitions demarcate thoughts across task contexts exposing the mental noise of trait neuroticism." *Nature Communications* 11 (2020).

Fogg, B.J. *Tiny Habits: The Small Changes that Change Everything.* Boston/New York: Houghton Mifflin Harcourt, 2020.

Chapter 5
Cherry, Kendra. Verywell Mind. "What Is the Negativity Bias?" https://www.verywellmind.com/negative-bias-4589618#where-negative-bias-comes-from

Loder, Vanessa. "The Power of Vision -- What Entrepreneurs Can Learn From Olympic Athletes." *Forbes,* July 23, 2014, https://www.forbes.com/sites/vanessaloder/2014/07/23/the-power-of-vision-what-entrepreneurs-can-learn-from-olympic-athletes/?sh=1aee8ae56e74

Chapter 8
Chowdhury, Madhuleena Roy. PositivePsychology.com. "The Neuroscience of Gratitude and How It Affects Anxiety & Grief," October 9, 2021.https://positivepsychology.com/neuroscience-of-gratitude/

Chapter 10

Barsade, Sigal. "The Contagion We Can Control." *Harvard Business Review,* March 26, 2020, https://hbr.org/2020/03/the-contagion-we-can-control

O, Brien, Pamela. Shape. "Here's How Working Out Can Make You More Resilient to Stress." July 28, 2020. https://www.shape.com/fitness/tips/exercise-mental-resilience-stress

Chapter 11

Raglio, Alfredo, Attardo, Lapo, Gontero, Giulia, Rollino, Silvia, Groppo, Elisabetta, Granieri, Enrico. "Effects of Music and Music Therapy on Mood in Neurological Patients." *World Journal of Psychiatry* 5, no.1 (March 2015): 68-78.

Ferguson, Yuna L. and Sheldon, Kennon M. "Trying to Be Happier Can Work: Two Experimental Studies." *The Journal of Positive Psychology* 8, no.1 (2013): 23-33.

FURTHER READING

These are some of the books from authors and speakers that have inspired me on my path. Check them out as you continue to expand and grow your mindset and possibilities.

The EQ Edge: Emotional Intelligence and your Success
by Steven J. Stein and Howard E. Book

Tiny Habits: The Small Changes that Change Everything
by B.J. Fogg

Awaken the Giant Within
by Tony Robbins

15 Secrets Successful People Know About Time Management
by Kevin Kruse

The Success Principles: How to Get from Where You are to Where You Want to Be
by Jack Canfield

Innercise: The New Science to Unlock Your Brain's Hidden Power
by John Assaraf

How to Win Friends and Influence People
by Dale Carnegie

Eat that Frog: Stop Procrastinating and Get More Done in Less Time
by Brian Tracy

The 4-Hour Workweek: Escape the 9-5, Live Anywhere and Join the New Rich
by Tim Ferris